Prepper Pantry

The Survival Guide to Modern Day Emergency Food & Water Storage

(Steps for Creating Long-term Storage to Survive Any Disaster)

John Welch

Published By **Elena Holly**

John Welch

Prepper Pantry: The Survival Guide to Modern Day Emergency Food & Water Storage (Steps for Creating Long-term Storage to Survive Any Disaster)

ISBN   978-1-998769-69-8

No part of this guidebook shall be reproduced in any form without permission in writing from the publisher except in the case of brief quotations embodied in critical articles or reviews.

Legal & Disclaimer

Table of contents

Chapter 1: Prepping Your Pantry

There are some ground rules which you need to be aware of in relation to stocking up your preppers pantry:

· Do now not select salty foods as these will cause thirst.

· Keep at the least a gallon of consuming water in step with day for each household member.

· Make the food equipped to consume so that you do no longer should dissipate gas or water in making ready them.

· Keep at the very least 3 days' worth of food and water for every household member.

· Do no longer forget about to percent meals and water to your pets.

· Include a primary useful resource kit to your meals pantry that carries OTC and prescription medication, in addition to a CPR face protect, antibiotic ointments, bandages and other simple medical materials.

It is likewise vital to be versatile in relation to food instruction in instances of crisis. Learn how to begin an open wood hearth. This will now not be hard when you have stored charcoal and/or dried timber and packing containers of fits to your pantry. You also can put money into a sun oven, a rocket range, or a volcano range to make cooking and boiling drinking water an less complicated system.

In assembling a preppers pantry, make sure that you have a meal planner to cautiously plot out right vitamins and hydration allocation for every family member. The ingredients which you ought to save need to offer for the electricity desires of each family member, especially at some stage in an emergency.

Are you geared up to start stocking up your preppers pantry? Read on.

Chapter 2: Water Purification And Storage

All preppers ought to recognize the guideline of 3 in survival. This way you can best live on up to 3 mins without a air, 3 hours and not using a safe haven, 3 days with out water, and 3 weeks without meals. In reality, if you are used to the comforts of contemporary life, you can final plenty much less than that, but don't be troubled for you can cope with considered one of the biggest worries in terms of your survival: potable water.

How to Find Drinking Water

Now is the time to set apart drinking water to your preppers pantry to your circle of relatives. However, in case you outlasted your deliver, you should understand where and how to accumulate water for ingesting.

The first step in doing that is to emerge as acquainted with your environment. Let us say your water supply at home suddenly runs dry. Can you cite approximately 5 other places where you may get sparkling water within a five-mile radius? If you don't, you should begin mapping it out right now. This can save your existence. Some viable sources are wells, lakes, streams, springs, herbal ponds and rivers.

Rainwater is a supply that you can resort to if all else fails. If feasible, you can also scavenge for bottled water in shops close to your place, but do now not depend an excessive amount of on this in the course of city emergencies due to the fact human beings will most likely wipe all of the shares out.

How to Purify Water

The second potable water turns into extremely scarce at some stage in urban emergencies, your survival abilities can be put to the check. If you have been able to gather water, but you accept as true with that it is not secure for consuming, you then have to learn how to purify it. You should additionally teach this ability to different own family participants so that they may be able to fend for themselves in case considered one of you is separated from the alternative.

Crude Filter

You can create a filter to do away with dust and different bodily contaminants out of your water. It is the first step to purification. To make your crude clear out, you may want a 1.5 or 2-liter soda bottle, a fabric-like clear out along with a cheesecloth or espresso filter, a cup of gravel, and half of a cup of sand and of charcoal.

Cut the bottom of the soda bottle to create a wide commencing so that it'd appear to be a funnel. Stuff the spout of the bottle with the cloth-like clear out or wrap it round from the out of doors and preserve it in location with some string or rubber bands. The first layer for your filter out will be the charcoal, accompanied by using the sand, after which the gravel.

To use the crude clear out, location it over a easy bucket. Gradually pour the water into the wide establishing and allow it trickle via the layers to filter out the debris. Catch the filtered water with the bucket.

Keep in mind that filtering by myself will not make the water potable. It will nevertheless contain the parasites and pathogens that are gift inside the water. Therefore, the subsequent step would be to purify it.

Boil

The oldest trick within the e-book of water purification is sincerely boiling. To make certain that the little residents for your water could be killed by the high temperature, ensure to boil it for about 5 to 12 mins. The horrific information is that boiling water can eat gas, so if you can not start a fire in an city emergency placing, then you have to do not forget the other purification techniques.

If boiling is the handiest way, you ought to placed a lid on your pot, bucket or some thing it is you are using to boil your water so that you can keep lots of the water and not lose it to evaporation.

Water Purification drugs

An essential addition in your preppers pantry should be water purification tablets or chlorine dioxide. Simply follow the manufacturer's commands and you are good to head.

Chlorine Bleach

The use of sodium hypochlorite, or in easy phrases your basic household (unscented) bleach, is a greater electricity-green alternative to purifying your water. Adding this to filtered water will the harmful pathogens and parasites which might be dwelling in it. All you need to do is add about a quarter of a teaspoon of chlorine bleach to each gallon of water. After that, you have to set it aside for half of an hour to present it time to do its work.

Iodine

Another opportunity is to apply 2 percent iodine tincture. Keep in mind that this is not an choice for pregnant women and for those who have clinical conditions along with thyroid troubles. However, in case you do not have a problem with iodine, then you can stock up on a 2 percentage iodine tincture in liquid or pill shape. Add about 8 drops of it per gallon of clean filtered water, or 16 drops consistent with gallon of cloudy water. This will kill most of the pathogens, however now not all of the damaging protozoa.

Once you have filtered and purified your water, ensure to keep them in included bins to prevent any particles and different overseas gadgets from going in and contaminating the water over again. As tons as possible, purify the water which you could most effective want for that day. This will assist decrease the expenditure of your purification supplies and make certain which you and your family may have freshly purified water each day.

Chapter 3: Food Preservation

Just because you are making ready your pantry for emergencies does now not suggest it have to include dangerous ingredients. While commercially preserved meals are the perfect route, they are usually chock full of preservatives and salt.

It would be an awesome idea to build up to your emergency meals garage gradually. You do no longer ought to do it multi function pass. For instance, you may begin buying an extra can of tuna every time you bear in mind buying one. You can also opt for MREs or Meals Ready to Eat which are vacuum-sealed meals used by the military. It would additionally be an awesome concept to save a few meal-alternative bars that include all the macro-nutrients that your body will want. Just pick the low-sodium ones.

Now here comes the amusing part: preparing your own preserved foods on your preppers pantry. There are 4 ways in doing that: home canning, dehydrating, freeze-drying, and vacuum packing.

Home Canning

You can store your own preserved food in sterilized jars and preserve them in your preppers pantry. What you do is kill the micro organism in the food with the aid of filing it to a high temperature. There are three techniques in canning your own meals, and these are thru water tub, pressure, and dry canning.

Dehydrating

This manner of preserving meals entails extracting all the liquid from your meals to lengthen its shelf lifestyles. After dehydrating, the food will then be vacuum-packed or dry canned. You will want a simple meals dehydrator for this.

Freeze-drying

You should buy freeze-dried ingredients, however in case you need to put together your own, you must keep in thoughts that it could be a piece highly-priced. The benefit of freezing your meals is it permits most retention of vitamins within the food, almost to the factor as if it's far sparkling.

Vacuum packing

This simple technique includes placing the food in a plastic bag, eliminating all of the air from inside and then sealing it to prolong its shelf existence.

You will find a wide style of smooth recipes that involve these strategies in the chapters that follow. Before getting ready anything, just make certain to create a meal planner to help you and your family control the meals for your preppers pantry and permit your components remaining long enough till assist arrives.

Chapter 4: Canning Fruits

Fruit is one of the simplest ingredients to can, which makes this the first food coaching ability that you can practice on for survival. Choose fruits that are in-season right earlier than you may them, in order that you'll be capable of maintain the high-quality dietary fee and taste.

The handiest special system you may need to can fruits is a canner, so ensure you have got that in conjunction with your jars, lids, and bands for storing the preserved fruits.

Here are recipes that you can follow. You can also use the same recipes for preserving different fruits which can be available domestically and are in-season on your location.

Blueberry Compote

· 1 cup water

· 2 cups granulated sugar

· 4 cups sparkling blueberries

· 1/6 cup lemon juice, clean or bottled

· 2 pint jars, lids, and bands

1.   Pour enough water into the canner to cowl the jars. Bring to a boil, then lower the heat and positioned the jars within the water. Let simmer. Simmer the bands and lids in a small skillet over low flame.

2. In a saucepan, blend the water and sugar. Bring to a boil and allow simmer for 5 minutes. Add the blueberries and simmer for about 5 minutes or till the blueberries come aside. Turn off the flame and add the lemon juice, stirring continuously.

three. Carefully take the sterilized jars out of the canner with a pair of tongs and pour the blueberry mixture into them. Make sure that there are not any air bubbles.

Wipe the rims smooth and put the lids at the center. Screw the bands on until they're tight.

four. Put the crammed jars lower back into the canner. Make sure that about an inch of water covers the jars. Bring to a boil and keep the temperature for approximately 10 mins. Then cast off the jars and set aside to chill earlier than storing.

Peach Preserves

· 6 lb peaches

· 2 1/2 cups water

· 1 1/four cups granulated sugar

· 2 quart jars, lids, and bands

1.   Pour simply sufficient water in the canner so that it will cowl the jars. Bring to a boil, then lower to low warmness. Carefully region the jars into the water and simmer. Sterilize the lids and bands as

nicely by using setting them in a saucepan with simmering water.

2. Boil a pot of water and placed the peaches into it. Boil for 30 seconds then right now take them out and transfer them right into a bowl full of extra bloodless water. This will assist you to take the skins off effortlessly. After skinning, slice them in half of and discard the pits.

3. Take the jars out of the canner with tongs. Transfer the peaches into the sterilized jars, but make certain to leave approximately half of an inch of space among the peaches and the outlet.

four. Combine the water and sugar in a skillet and convey to a boil, stirring continuously. Pour the syrup over the peaches. Make certain to leave 1/2 inch of space.

5. Remove the air bubbles, wipe the rims, location the lids on pinnacle and tighten

the bands. Put the crammed jars lower back into the canner, making sure that they're absolutely submerged with about an inch of water above the lids. Boil for 25 minutes, then cautiously take the jars out and set them aside to cool before storing.

Chapter 5: Pickles

The process of pickling has been practiced for hundreds of years, mainly in elements of the world wherein people could still like to revel in veggies and fruits at some point of the wintertime.

During city emergencies, you truely could want to have jars of pickles to your preppers pantry. Here are a few simple recipes on how to put together your own at domestic.

Spicy Pickled Okra

· 1 lb fresh young okra

· three Tbsp pickling salt

· 1/2 quart white vinegar

· four cloves garlic, chopped

· 8 clean warm peppers

· 1/eight cup entire dill seed

· 1/8 cup entire mustard seed

· three pint jars, lids, and bands

1.   Boil sufficient water within the canner to submerge the jars completely. Once it begins to boil, decrease the warmth and carefully positioned the jars internal. Let simmer. Sterilize the lids and bands in a saucepan full of simmering water over medium-low warmth.

2. Wash the okra, then snip off the stems, however go away the caps. Soak them in a bowl of icy bloodless water for 60 minutes, then pat dry.

3. In a non-metallic pot, blend the vinegar, garlic, salt, mustard seed, dill seed, and warm peppers. Bring to a boil and allow simmer for 5 mins.

four. Transfer the okra into the jars after which fill it with the recent liquid aggregate. Make certain to depart approximately 1/2 an inch of space among the contents and the outlet of the jars.

5. Remove the air bubbles, wipe the edges, connect the lids and screw the bands on till tight. Put the jars into the canner, ensuring that there is about an inch of area masking the lids. Bring to a boil and hold the temperature for 10 mins. Then carefully take the jars out and set aside to cool.

6. If you are planning to devour the produce, simplest do so after four weeks to permit it undergo the pickling method first.

Pickled Beets

· five lb beets

· 2 1/2 cups white vinegar

· half Tbsp pickling salt

· 1 1/four cups granulated sugar

· 2 half of Tbsp complete cloves

· 3 quart jars, lids, and bands

1.   Boil just enough water within the canner to cowl the jars. Once boiling, put the heat on low then cautiously region the jars into the water. Let simmer. Sterilize the lids and bands in simmering water in a saucepan over low warmness.

2. Put the beets in a big pot and fill with water. Boil for about 15 minutes or till smooth, then cautiously get rid of the pot from the warmth source and set apart to chill. Once cool enough to deal with, peel the beets. If the beets you're the usage of are large, you may slice them.

3. In a nonreactive saucepan, combine the other ingredients. Place over high flame and convey to a boil. Then, set apart.

4. Take the jars out of the canners and positioned the beets into them, making

sure that they may be no longer squished in the procedure. Pour the new liquid into the jar. Make certain to go away about an inch of space among the contents and the jar commencing. Add a clove to every jar.

five. Get rid of any air bubbles, wipe the edges, put the lids on, and then screw the bands on tight. Put the jars back into the canner, making sure that the jars are absolutely submerged with over an inch of water above them. Boil for 15 mins, then carefully take them out and set them apart to cool before storing.

Chapter 6: Pressure Canning

The first-rate way to maintain greens, chicken, meats and seafood is by way of stress canning. Since these ingredients are low acid, you can't sincerely can them within the traditional sense.

To get you began on strain canning on your preppers pantry, you may want the following:

1. Dial-gauge or weighted-strain canner

2. Rack for the pressure canner

3. Tongs for lifting jars

4. Jars, new lids, and bands

five. Canning funnel

6. Clean dish towels, a few for wiping, others for cooling the jars

7. A skinny spatula or butter knife

eight. A timer

nine.   Some labels and a marker

Once you have those gear, you may start pressure canning! Make positive to examine the recipe and apprehend each step completely before intending. That manner, you will be successful.

Pressure Canned Corn

· 10 freshly picked ears of corn, de-husked

· 2 tsp salt

· four pints jars, lids, and bands

1.   Boil the jars in a large pot. Once boiling, positioned heat on low and allow simmer. Sterilize the lids and bands in simmering water over low heat.

2. Fill the strain canner with 3 inches of water and bring to a boil.

3. Fill any other pot with water and convey to a boil. Blanch the complete ears of corn within the boiling water for three minutes,

then right away switch them right into a bowl of icy bloodless water.

four. Cut off the kernels from the corn the use of a sharp knife or corn cobber, making sure not to scrape the cob. Transfer the kernels right into a massive bowl.

5. Boil water in a massive pot and preserve it boiling as you pour the corn into the jars. Make certain to go away approximately an inch of space between the jar lid and the corn. Add half a teaspoon of salt into every jar after which pour the boiling water over the corn, still leaving an inch of space.

6. Get rid of any air bubbles, wipe the rims dry, attach the lids, and screw the bands on tight. Put the jars in the canner.

7. Cover, vent, and then pressurize the canner based totally at the manufacturer's instructions. Process for about 55 minutes

at eleven lb of strain. After that, you could take the canner off the heat supply and set aside to chill before you remove the jars.

Pressure Canned Green Beans

· 7 lb inexperienced beans

· three half of tsp salt

· 7 pint jars, lids, and bands

1.   Boil the jars in a large pot. After it starts offevolved to boil, decrease heat and let simmer. Sterilize the lids and bands by way of covering them with water and simmering them over a low flame.

2. Fill the strain canner with three inches of water and area over high warmness.

three. Pour water into every other pot and produce to a boil. Meanwhile, wash the green beans, snip off the ends, and take away the strings.

4. Take the jars out of the pot and region the beans into them, making sure to depart an inch of space between the beans and the outlet of the jar. Pour in only sufficient boiling water to cover the beans.

5. Divide the salt between the jars, wipe the rims dry, placed the lids on, and tighten the bands. Put the jars into the stress canner, cover, vent, and pressurize. Cook for 20 minutes at 11 lb of pressure, then get rid of the canner from the flame and set apart to cool earlier than storing the jars.

Pressure Canned Mushrooms and Onions

· 2 lb mushrooms, sliced

· 7 medium-length onions, skinned, sliced, and reduce into jewelry

· 1 Tbsp salt

· 4 quart jars, lids, and bands

1.   Sterilize the jars, lids, and bands by way of boiling the jars in a pot complete of water and placing the lids and bands in a saucepan of gently simmering water.

2. Fill the pressure canner with three inches of water and bring to a boil. Blanch the onions and mushrooms for five minutes, then positioned them within the jars. Divide the salt between the jars. Make certain that there's half of an inch of area within the jar.

3. Remove the air bubbles, wipe the edges dry, positioned the lids on, and tighten with the bands. Put the jars into the canner, cowl, vent and pressurize.

four. Cook for half of an hour at 11 lb of strain, then take away the canner from the heat and set apart to chill earlier than storing the jars.

Chicken Soup

- 8 cups chook inventory

- 1 1/2 cups diced cooked hen

- 3/4 cup sliced carrots

- three/four cup diced celery

- half cup diced onion

- 1 tsp salt

- half of tsp freshly ground black pepper

- 1/four cup chopped sparkling parsley

- 1 Tbsp chopped sparkling thyme

- three/four tsp floor turmeric

- 2 quart jars, lids, and bands

- Chicken bouillon cubes

1.   Boil the jars in a huge pot. After it begins to boil, decrease heat and allow simmer. Sterilize the lids and bands by way of masking them with water and simmering them over a low flame.

2. Fill the stress canner with three inches of water and place over high warmth.

3. Mix the fowl, bird stock, carrots, onion, and celery in a pot over medium-excessive flame. Let boil, then decrease warmness to medium. Season with the parsley, thyme, turmeric, salt, and pepper. Stir to combine. Let simmer for 30 minutes and add the bouillon cubes.

4. Divide the soup among the jars, making sure to go away an inch of space. Get rid of any air bubbles, wipe the edges dry, and tighten with the bands. Put the jars into the canner, cowl, vent and pressurize.

5. Cook for ninety mins at 10 lb of strain. Take the canner off the warmth and permit cool before storing the jars.

Vegetable Soup

· 3 cups sliced carrots

· 3 cups peeled and diced potatoes

· 4 cups green beans, trimmed and sliced into 1 inch pieces

· four cups peeled and chopped tomatoes

· 2 cups uncooked corn kernels

· 1 cup 1 inch sliced celery

· 1 cup chopped yellow onions

· 3 cups water

· 1 tsp salt

· 1/2 tsp freshly floor black pepper

· 1/four cup chopped sparkling parsley

· half Tbsp chopped fresh rosemary

· 4 quart jars, lids, and bands

1.   Sterilize the jars, lids, and bands via boiling the jars in a pot complete of water and placing the lids and bands in a saucepan of gently simmering water.

2. Fill the stress canner with three inches of water and place over high warmth.

three. Mix the water, salt, pepper, and all the vegetables in a pot and positioned over medium-excessive heat. Add the herbs and stir to combine. Bring to a boil, then placed heat on medium-low and let simmer for 20 mins.

four. Divide the soup among the jars making sure that there may be an inch of area left. Get rid of any air bubbles, wipe the edges dry, attach the lids, and tighten with the bands.

five. Put the jars into the canner, cover, vent and pressurize. Cook for approximately an hour and 25 minutes at 10 lb pressure. Remove the canner from the flame and set aside to cool before storing.

Chapter 7: Drying Food

Many human beings use the process of drying meals for the duration of the centuries, particularly when it comes to finishing their food components. You also can make your personal dried meals at home and fill up your preppers pantry with them. To make this a handy technique for you, you should buy an lower priced and efficient food dehydrator.

Once you have a food dehydrator, you may without a doubt follow the manufacturer's commands on how to function it. Just preserve in mind the following hints:

Drying Vegetables

Drying veggies is pretty smooth. The vegetables usually grow to be searching like chips and are easy to save and eat up for the duration of an emergency. Here are a few standard pointers:

· Make certain to scrub your vegetables properly with cold water after which cut off any stems before dehydrating.

· When drying beets, broccoli and cauliflower, reduce them up into 1/four inch pieces earlier than drying and process them from three to 10 hours, 4 to 10 hours, and six to fourteen hours, respectively.

· Blanch green beans and peas before drying and system them in the dehydrator for 6 to 12 hours.

· Shred or slice carrots before dehydrating. Process for 6 to twelve hours.

· Corn needs to be de-husked, washed, blanched and the kernels must be removed from the cob before drying.

Spread the kernels out on a sheet and method for six to twelve hours.

· Slice the potatoes and zucchini into extra-thin pieces and procedure for 6 to 12 hours and five to ten hours, respectively.

· Boil, peel and slice tomatoes before drying. Process for six to 12 hours.

Drying Fruits - Fruit Leather

The first-class way to shop dried foods is in a freezer. However, if you need to put together for city emergencies that encompass strength outages which can be probably to occur in such situations, then you may make fruit leather-based.

How to make Fruit Leather

· Fresh fruit of your preference (which include apples, peaches, grapes, plums)

· Water

· Optional: Granulated sugar

· Lemon juice

· Spices (such as floor cinnamon and nutmeg)

1.   Preheat the dehydrator to one hundred fifty tiers F.

2. Wash, rinse, and cut off the cores, stems, peels, and pits of the fruit. Add sugar, but if the fruit is already candy, there may be no want for this.

3. Put the fruit into a saucepan and add approximately half of a cup of water for every four cups of chopped fruit. Let simmer, cowl, and prepare dinner over low flame.

4. Uncover and stir, then overwhelm the fruit the usage of a potato masher or a meals processor. Add lemon juice and spices in small amounts and flavor the mixture to regulate. Process till easy.

5. Put the mashed fruit lower back into the saucepan and simmer, stirring constantly, until thickened.

6. Line a baking sheet with a microwavable plastic wrap. Pour the pureed fruit into it to a thickness of about 1/4 inch or much less. Put the sheet into the dehydrator for 8 to 10 hours or until dry. The fruit leather need to be clean and no longer sticky. Peel the plastic wrap off and save it in an hermetic field within the freezer.

Drying Meats

Always dry the meat at one hundred forty levels F whilst using the dehydrator. Follow the encouraged time. Make certain that the inner temperature of the beef is one hundred sixty ranges F. You can check that by using the usage of one piece from a batch as the "pattern". It ought to be especially thicker than the rest of the portions. If the thermometer displays that temperature in this piece, then the relaxation are safe to save.

Here are two simple and easy dried-meat recipes that you could follow:

Beef Jerky

· 8 oz.Worcestershire sauce

· 8 ouncessoy sauce

· 1 tsp garlic powder

· 1 tsp onion powder

· half of tsp freshly ground black pepper

· Optional: half tsp cayenne pepper, half tsp crimson pepper flakes

· 2 lb lean pork, thinly sliced with the grain

1.   Combine the spices and sauces in a blending bowl and then add the beef. Coat all of the pieces in the combination. Refrigerate for twenty-four hours. Stir every so often.

2. Dry for 12 hours or primarily based on the dehydrator's instructions. The meat should be very dry. This recipe makes half a pound of red meat jerky.

Turkey Jerky

· 1 half tsp lemon juice

· 8 oz.Soy sauce

· 1 tsp cracked black pepper

· 1 tsp powdered garlic

· 1/2 tsp ground ginger

· half tsp onion powder

· 2 lb boneless, skinless turkey breast, trimmed and sliced 1/4 inch thick with the grain

1. Combine the moist ingredients with the spices in a blending bowl. Add the turkey breast and blend to mix.

Refrigerate for 24 hours, stirring once in a while.

2. Arrange in a unmarried layer at the dehydrator tray and system for 8 hours at a hundred forty five levels F. This recipe makes half of a pound of turkey jerky.

The Three Pillars of Surviving a Disaster

After analyzing numerous survival cases and stories, researchers have come to the realization that there are 3 major pillars that determine success. The first pillar is get admission to to the elements whilst the catastrophe happens. This consists of both the materials which you stocked up on and the substances on your surrounding region. The second factor is the extent of your survival knowledge. Having get entry to to components and equipment will most effective increase your survival timeframe for see you later before you run out of elements or make a mistake. Individuals who are experienced and understand the way to live on will outlast their opposite numbers who best have access to primary substances, supplies, and know-how. Finally, the 0.33 factor is the sheer will to live to tell the tale. There were numerous stories of survival regardless of insurmountable odds, solely due to the fact the survivor had the desire to stay. The trick to maximizing your survival time is to grasp every of those 3 elements and restrict your weaknesses.

Access to Equipment and Supplies

This is one aspect in order to maximum possibly be underneath your control unless an unexpected catastrophe takes place whilst you are far from home and without a survival trojan horse out package. By preserving your private home and computer virus out car nicely provided at all times you can relaxation confident that you will be prepared for maximum disasters. There is always the opportunity of an outlier catastrophe, which leaves your property and automobile destroyed – in which case you'll want to work along with your surroundings. However, there may be no excuse to no longer to have the right survival elements and trojan horse out kit available in your private home.

Following this e book and making sure that you have a right food and water storage machine in place should be your first step. Relying on stores and the infrastructure of your nearby government may be a fatal mistake. Being able to survive without counting on shops is a significant benefit and permits you to avoid venturing out. When food and water come to be scarce, violence fast erupts and you may locate yourself in a very tough situation. Stocking up and warding off these situations is imperative to make sure your survival for an prolonged time period.

The very last step is to ensure you have the right device for both a computer virus out scenario and a hunker down scenario. Many preppers make the error of stocking up on handiest food and water and averting spending the extra time on survival equipment. Water filters, flashlights, generators, cooking device, clinical supplies, etc. Are all vital to extend your survival timeline. Having a cache of these substances in each your own home and trojan horse out places are crucial. By ensuring you have got all 3 of those factors protected, you'll be a long way extra superior than many beginner preppers.

Knowledge

Another not unusual mistake among preppers is ordering big quantities of gadget with little to no actual know-how of the way to use it. Please do no longer count on that simply because you purchased the encouraged equipment, you're organized for any catastrophe. Most equipment no longer most effective takes time however also practice to hone and turn out to be proficient with the tool. Learning on the fly for the duration of a disaster will not handiest cause damaged tools and much frustration, however it may additionally be downright risky.

The simple way to keep away from this problem is to make sure you have experience with your gear earlier than a disaster occurs. Take time to practice heating and cooking outdoors with the family. Learn how to properly filter water. Learn the fine details of your generator and a way to well keep it. These are all sports that take little or no time, and you may quickly locate yourself acquiring the knowledge to master those tools at some point of a catastrophe.

Just the information of how to properly use your gear throughout a catastrophe isn't enough to noticeably make bigger your survival odds, but. You need to study primary survival strategies inclusive of starting a hearth, recuperation wounds, looking, and many others. These talents will diversify your abilties and assist you to survive regardless of the system or scenario which you locate your self in.

The Will to Survive

The final survival thing we're going to discuss is the need to live on. The will to live on is frequently considered the defining thing in relation to survival. Yes, you locate your self in a tough state of affairs, now what are you going to do about it? There are numerous notable survival testimonies about castaways lost at sea for months, rock climbers who amputated their own fingers, or army seals faced with insurmountable odds yet surviving. Survival isn't smooth by any approach and your will to continue to exist may be the very last aspect that determines whether or not you give up or live to see every other day.

Mental toughness is a skill that can be honed and developed over the years. The navy and army spend hours training and developing the mental durability in their new recruits. There are loads of army seals that don't make the reduce each yr regardless of their bodily health. The distinction is the intellectual durability and will to be successful. Separating the mentally and physically hard crowd from folks who most effective have the bodily staying power is vital to education and developing the brand new class of seals and rangers.

While you don't want to undergo navy seal training to expand your intellectual toughness, we do suggest you exercise a few physical games. Try camping for a few days with only your survival equipment. Try to create situations where you simulate survival situations. The more often you simulate these events, the greater cushty you'll sense during a catastrophe. Shock and tension are often very high immediately following a disaster, which reasons many people to truely surrender or not take any movement. By slowly schooling your self to show intellectual readability and hone your will to live to tell the tale, you may discover yourself in lots higher form than most those who are used to sitting at the sofa and watching television.

Later on in this book we will discuss the importance of consolation food and why you ought to pay close interest to storing those gadgets. Most dehydrated and freeze-dried ingredients lack the flavor of ordinary foods. After weeks of ingesting into your food supply you may fast locate that morale starts offevolved to drop off. Having comfort food is critical to maintain your family, in particular the small survivors, glad. Happy humans have a far stronger will to continue to exist. We advocate you get used to the flavor and texture of survival meals by way of periodically cooking a survival meal on your circle of relatives.

Ten Points of Stress During a Disaster

During a disaster you'll be now not simplest bodily careworn but mentally exhausted as nicely. Understanding in which those strain points occur and the way to for my part address each one will assist you to always preserve your will to live. Many humans sense stress and understand the idea as a huge time period.

This makes pressure hard to handle and reasons it to appear to be an amazing opponent. However, if you can smash down and awareness on every character factor of stress you may be able to take care of and overcome it.

Stress Point #1: Fear

The human reaction to any kind of disaster is fear. Fear comes from the natural reaction to uncertainty and the hazard of risk. Your body will be generating adrenaline, in an effort to hold you extensive awake at night and give you the power to stay alert. Unfortunately, a loss of sleep and the general strain that adrenaline locations for your frame makes it less than ideal as a protracted-time period solution. You will fast experience burnt out and confused out. Your questioning may additionally become cloudy and you may suffer from fatigue.

Solution: the great manner to fight an inflow of adrenaline and strain is to make certain you are napping and ingesting the proper quantities. Staying wakeful all night and slightly consuming are ways to get your self in problem straight away. Even if it's almost not possible to doze off, you must lie as still as feasible or attempt to meditate to allow your thoughts to relax. If you are suffering to preserve food down you must try eating small quantities of high calorie foods such as peanut butter. A few spoonfuls will offer your frame as a minimum some of the nourishment it wishes to make clean and concise selections.

Stress Point #2: Pain

Injuries and pain are commonplace for the duration of most failures. You might also have sustained an injury all through the disaster or whilst you have been escaping. With adrenaline flowing through your frame, you may now not word your injury till you sooner or later get a threat to relax. This is while the battle in opposition to pain begins. Injuries, cuts, and wounds that are not dealt with immediately are at risk of contamination and you'll locate your self struggling with pain day in and day out.

Solution: make sure you've got medical supplies to your worm out bag and on your hunker down place. Learn on-the-fly medical techniques to stop bleeding and disinfect wounds. Having even a basic expertise of ache and scientific treatment is essential. Keep ache medicinal drug available always if possible in the course of a catastrophe.

Stress Point #3: Illness

With a depleted immune system and shortage of right sanitation you will conflict with closing healthful for lengthy intervals of time. Common illnesses that may be cured with medicine in a functioning society can quickly grow to be fatal when you are in a disaster scenario. The close proximity on your other survival buddies and the spread of food-borne illnesses will make it difficult to stay healthful if you aren't careful.

Solution: ensure you are taking the right steps to ensure you are following proper sanitation technique. Clean and disinfect all of your equipment and avoid food-borne ailments in any respect costs. Don't eat or drink something that you feel might be even barely contaminated. "Better secure than sorry" need to be your motto in case you need to keep away from getting unwell and risking your probabilities for survival.

Stress Point #four: Heat

Heat exhaustion is a actual hazard, specially if you stay in a hot weather. The lack of aircon and color could make it pretty uncomfortable for lengthy periods of time. Excessive sweating can result in speedy dehydration and staying cool fast will become vital. Prolonged warmth can agitate even the calmest humans and tempers will quickly upward thrust as the heat index actions higher.

Solution: drink sufficient water and recognize how to preserve the limited water you have got handy. Additionally, ensure you've got at the least a fundamental expertise of the way to create shelter when the warmth will become too unbearable. Understanding how to hold cool in a warm surroundings is essential to maintaining your frame and your mindset cool.

Stress Point #5: Cold

Staying heat with out strength in a humid and bloodless surroundings is another venture you need to prepare for while a catastrophe does occur. Just because you live in a heat weather doesn't mean you shouldn't prepare for bloodless weather. Remember there are four seasons every yr and you have to put together similarly for all 4. A disaster is simply as in all likelihood to occur in the summertime as it is within the iciness.

Solution: gain proper heating device in your own home and you've proper fireplace-starting gadget to your computer virus out bag. You should be well versed in starting a fire and your worm out bag must preserve one-of-a-kind changes of clothes. One hassle that many preppers face is they invent a bug out bag but they don't rotate or trade the equipment. This can lead to suffering if you have flawed seasonal clothes. Taking the time to make certain both your property and bug out baggage are prepared for the current season can be the difference between lifestyles and demise.

Stress Point #6: Sleep Deprivation

The survival charge for preppers typically drops dramatically at the five to seven day mark at the disaster timeline. At this point you have had little to no sleep and your frame has begun to get used to the excess adrenaline. Sleep deprivation starts offevolved to kick in and your concept system begins to cloud. Sleep deprivation is very dangerous and it is able to be tough to understand the symptoms when you are already laid low with exhaustion. Sleep deprivation will lead you to start taking useless risks and making rash decisions. You will be easily pissed off, that can make teamwork a massive trouble, mainly in case you are working with different preppers who are sleep deprived as nicely.

Sleep deprivation also inhibits your will to stay and can reason you to give up.

Solution: despite the fact that it is able to be extremely hard to nod off at night time, you want to relaxation your thoughts for at the least some hours. Learning a way to meditate is very useful that will help you relieve stress and provide your thoughts the relaxation it wishes. When running low on sleep, you must keep strength drinks and espresso at your disposal. Both will provide a cheap enhance of electricity in case you want to assume actually or accomplish a widespread goal. While coffee and energy drinks are vital, please do no longer underestimate the need for at least some hours of rest every night time.

Stress Point #7: Boredom

Boredom typically units in a few days after your adrenaline ranges go back to everyday. The days after a catastrophe can speedy emerge as recurring and dull as you wait for a rescue group or preserve to experience out the disaster. Life with out electricity may be more and more hard, specifically with modern-day reliance on cellular phones and video video games. Boredom can be quite a trouble, specially for more youthful survivors who lack the electricity and endurance to help out.

Solution: make sure your day is packed with activities to preserve your mind off boredom. Have the younger preppers help and strive your first-rate to preserve their minds active and stimulated. The minute they don't have something to accomplish, they'll quickly lose interest. Keep a % of gambling cards in all your bug out and survival caches. Hone your mind to those survival situations through taking weekend tenting trips and forbidding energy. This will assist you to test out your thoughts and unique methods to address boredom all through a survival state of affairs.

Stress Point #8: Loneliness

There is not any guarantee that if you survive you may be in a set with other survivors. Most people assume they will be able to live on with the organization of others. While running with others does have its advantages, it additionally has its downsides. You should be organized for each scenarios, and this means you should be organized to deal with loneliness. Extended intervals of time with out human interplay can quick result in melancholy. Once again, this will have an unfavorable affect on your potential and could to live to tell the tale. Learning how to cope with loneliness is essential to surviving lengthy timeframes without the touch of other human beings.

Solution: mastering the way to be alone for prolonged durations of time is critical to warfare loneliness. Some humans can not be on my own for hours, not to mention days. The idea of touring with out some other man or women terrifies some human beings, but surviving on your personal is a ability that desires to be honed and developed. Being on your personal and accountable for simplest yourself is a freeing feeling and may simply create a bit of a high. Travel to new locations by myself or pass tenting for extended durations of time by way of your self to domesticate this talent. You can also discover an inner peace and a new feel of confidence that you in no way concept existed.

Stress Point #nine: Hunger

Even when you have a nicely-stocked food supply, you will want to ration or at least reduce down on the quantity of calories you normally consume. This can be intricate for the ones people who like cake and other luxuries. The first few weeks might be the most tough as your body adjusts to the lowered wide variety of calories. This can lead to starvation pains and fatigue. Worse, if you don't have proper get right of entry to to food you will really suffer. So ensure your bug out bag and meals stockpile are nicely prepared to deal with the shortage of deliver all through a disaster. Don't rely upon the authorities!

Solution: make certain you have got sufficient food in your home meals storage machine to final the time frame of most screw ups. Also, make sure you have access to a properly stocked computer virus out bag inside the occasion you need to evacuate. Learning a way to cook your food supply is likewise important to surviving. Learning how to farm and hunt is also a vital talent if the disaster threatens society as an entire. Start small and start to train your self slowly till you can master every of those tasks.

Stress Point #10: Thirst

The identical point that we emphasised above applies in your water storage as well. One mistake that many preppers make is underestimating the amount of water their family consumes all through per week. This is just one motive we suggest monitoring your weekly water quantities so you have as a minimum an idea of how a lot water you want. Lack of water can quick flip deadly, specifically in case you are in a hot and dry environment.

Solution: make sure you have got sufficient water in your home and in your worm out bag. Water can be heavy and hard to carry, so make certain you are acquainted with water filters. Rain catchers are also necessary in case you are going to live on for long time frames in an city surroundings. Water purification strategies also are crucial to make certain you have got get entry to to water resources that aren't contaminated.

Infrastructure Collapse and How Your Food and Water Supply Can Save Your Life

As a society, we are very aware of using Amazon Prime to get our applications in forty eight hours, our grocery shops being properly stocked, and always gaining access to scientific components. We take as a right that our infrastructure machine will usually be in place and even if disrupted, it's going to quickly be repaired. This underestimation can cause trouble for almost all of the country, especially folks who lack proper water and food materials. All we ought to do is look at beyond screw ups to recognise that it may be weeks or months before help arrives. These are also isolated screw ups and should a comprehensive and coordinated assault occur, our infrastructure machine may be broken past repair. So permit's check the how fast our infrastructure system can disintegrate and why you have to continually be organized with proper meals and water components.

Timeline: 24-48 After Disaster

All submit places of work will close, mail routes will prevent, and your applications will be not on time. Since maximum first-world international locations run on "just-in-time" deliveries maximum groceries shops will start to revel in shortages of meals and water. Unless the shop turned into looted, there would possibly nonetheless be a few supplies last after forty eight hours. All manufacturers that require just-in-time deliveries can even stop to preserve operating. Most clinical facilities and hospitals will start to run out of materials, particularly if the disaster caused many injuries.

Timeline: three-5 Days After Disaster

Larger transportation of products will stall. Ships and trains will sit down idle or might be looted for materials. Garbage and sanitation problems begin to get up. Urban environments will enjoy considerable issues with sanitation on streets, as rubbish will not be collected. Gas stations may be low on or out of gas. Transportation and evacuation at this time frame turns into hard if no longer not possible. ATMs and banks may also be walking short on cash withdrawals. These limits can cause ruin on banks and looting will start in areas subsequent to banks. The necessities will disappear from grocery shops and all ultimate items will be looted. Consumer panic may additionally start, specifically if there is no phrase on re-components or authorities resource.

Timeline: 7-10 Days After Disaster

Hospitals will run out of most clinical components. Oxygen will become scarce and difficult choices will need to be made on patient priorities. All transportation will stop to feature because of lack of gasoline. Gasoline will speedy end up a hot barter item, especially to the ones who've get right of entry to to generators. Stores right now will quickly be looted. Homes which are suspected of having elements can even emerge as goals. Hunger and thirst will gas violence and law enforcement might be unfold thin. The feeling shifts from a central authority-run society to each guy for himself.

Timeline: 14-21 Days

Violence maintains to erupt, as medical, food, water, and gasoline resources are all dry. A "shoot first ask questions 2nd" version of survival is commonplace. Survivor groups form and being at the outdoor may be very risky. People start to suffer from starvation, which makes them even more determined to feed themselves and their households. Homes which are abandoned may be looted and domestic invasions become extra common. The buildup of garbage and sanitation makes clean consuming water not possible to locate. Casualty rates spike as residents begin drinking infected water or start to suffer from dehydration in dry areas.

Timeline: One Month

Gastrointestinal illnesses will retain to plague survivors, as easy water assets are nearly all long past. A weakened immune machine manner small injuries and cuts can become infected and purpose demise. Even those with a meals supply at the moment are beginning to reduce on intake. Seeking out extra assets of meals speedy becomes a concern which provides any other chance of leaving your compound. Urban environments are extremely hard to stay in, and therefore many human beings will start transferring out to surrounding regions. This results in an boom in domestic looting and casualties.

The above is a situation that now not best cuts off the nations infrastructure, however also includes the failure of presidency aid. This form of catastrophe is extraordinarily rare, but that doesn't mean you shouldn't be prepared for something like this to take place. Even in an event like Hurricane Katrina, it took weeks for government resource to attain the people. Being capable of live to tell the tale for extended intervals of time without resource from infrastructure or the authorities should be your principal difficulty when you are building your food and water substances.

This scenario is supposed to emphasise how speedy matters can turn for the worst throughout a catastrophe. The infrastructure we've in region ought to not be taken as a right, and you can see brief glimpses of its shortcomings all through hurricanes and effective wintry weather storms. The truth is that most international locations run on simply-in-time components and maintain most effective sufficient inventory to supply an afternoon's well worth of requirements for customers. Any hiccup inside the way this system works can quick cause problems and you need to ensure you're organized!

Why You Should Prepare

Whether you accept as true with that the arena is currently a secure place or you consider that the arena could quit quickly, you must as a minimum have a basic knowledge of what to do whilst a disaster does occur. Many individuals view preppers as conspiracy theorists or slightly delusional, however this couldn't be further from the fact. Preppers are organized for any sort of catastrophe, ranging from commonplace herbal disasters to unlikely large scale activities. They're organized and they recognize a way to take action in any of those conditions. How plenty you make a decision to prep is up to you, but having an information of this facts and being able to utilize these techniques should mean the difference between existence and dying.

The Increasing Volatility of Natural Disasters

Natural screw ups ought to be the primary motive you start to prep. From floods, fires, tornadoes, hurricanes, and earthquakes, regardless of wherein you stay, herbal screw ups can have an effect on you. Global warming and climate modifications have created more potent, powerful, and large herbal screw ups. Understanding how to defend your circle of relatives at some stage in and after these disasters is a ability that everyone have to possess. The survival charges throughout Hurricanes Katrina and Sandy might have been higher if those principals had been understood and practiced.

The Increasing Volatility of Man Made Disasters

While artifical disasters, like terrorism and struggle, are less in all likelihood than herbal failures, that doesn't mean you shouldn't be organized. Nuclear, biological, and chemical weapons are being advanced all through exceptional international locations, some of which might be taken into consideration terrorist international locations. Not to say gun violence and shootings were all over the headlines inside the news. Should those worse case situations occur, your information of prepping might be examined.

Common Occurrences During a Disaster

Unfortunately, many humans will depend on government resource and education during a disaster. The fact of the scenario is that the government might not be capable of offer aid until weeks right into a disaster. Finally, whilst aid comes it can now not be what you anticipate. Nothing is greater demoralizing then starving for weeks most effective for the government to show up with rationed food and water. Look at Hurricane Katrina as an instance of presidency resource and intervention. For weeks citizens needed to cope with aggressive violence, no meals and water, and horrible sanitation situations.

Stores fast ran out of meals and water, as any substances were quick looted. Violence speedy broke out as people turned on every other searching out substances. Others prevented hassle anticipating the authorities aid which took weeks to reach. Many casualties could have been averted if only a fundamental knowledge of prepping turned into understood.

The Breakdown of Violence

Many of you have got heard of the 80/20 percentage rule usually known as the Pareto major. Well, there's a similar rule that may be carried out to screw ups. This rule is taken into consideration the eighty/10/10 percent rule. The rule states that 80 percentage of people will do not anything in the course of a disaster. They're both paralyzed through fear, or they are awaiting a person to step up as a pacesetter. These are the folks that will live put in their houses irrespective of how horrific their state of affairs will become. The majority of those 80 percentage will rely upon authorities aid for meals and refuge. They have little to no understanding of survival capabilities and their odds of survival will depend upon others.

The subsequent 10 percentage resort to violence. Whether they're taking gain of a loss of law enforcement or they are simply scared and react with violence, these 10 percentage are the troublemakers. You will see this institution rioting and looting after or once in a while at some point of a catastrophe. They will shape "gangs" in the course of failures and raid homes looking for resources and valuables. This institution is responsible for all of the violence and looting of evacuated homes during hurricane Katrina and Hurricane Sandy.

The final 10% are the leaders and the folks who are organized for the state of affairs. They have a supply of all of the essential gadgets and information to continue to exist and assist others survive. These people are answerable for heroic acts and are frequently instances main the 80 percentage who're paralyzed by means of worry. They have the knowledge to treat medical troubles, have the resources to aid others, and feature the knowledge to lead different to protection. This expertise can come from military schooling, law enforcement information, or an know-how of prepping and survival talents. These ten percent are the real heroes and are accountable for saving lives.

Nations Run On Just In Time Supplies

It's not unusual know-how that almost all advanced nations run on "simply in time" deliveries. What this indicates is that food, water, and different materials are typically brought every day that allows you to stay fresh and preserved. Super markets handiest have sufficient inventory for twenty-four-48hrs. Even worse, whilst a catastrophe does occur many humans panic and begin to "stock up" despite the fact that they have to already have a right meals and water stockpile. This manner meals and sources are depleted nearly right now. You need with the intention to live to tell the tale those disaster situations and learn how to live to tell the tale with out relying on others for help.

Always Be Ready

You in no way recognize when or wherein a disaster will strike, so you continually need to be prepared. Disasters can occur in a split second, and your survival price will lower every second you waste trying to initiate your survival plan. You need to be geared up, no matter in case you are at work, faculty, or relaxing on the weekend.

Stores Cannot Be Relied On

Once a disaster takes place you need to have your own deliver of meals, water, and survival equipment. Stores will fast sell out of resources or they'll be quickly looted. Trying to buy last minute substances can put you in damage's way. We will go into detail inside the next few chapters on how you can construct a supply of everything needed to continue to exist for an prolonged period of time.

Government Aid

Government useful resource is also a luxurious that you shouldn't depend on. As we stated above, it can take the authorities weeks to offer resource to victims. In a full scale disaster, you want to be conscious that the government might not be coming or providing any aid. When aid does display up, it could be rationed without sufficient food and water to supply your circle of relatives. You want to learn how to offer meals, shelter, and protection to you and your own family. You want to emerge as self-enough and rely best on yourself when a catastrophe does arise.

It's Okay to Start Small

We are going to be presenting you with numerous lists of substances, device, and essentials in this e-book. Some of these items are cheaper, even as different can convey pretty the charge tag. Some readers can also feel stress and tension as they are now not properly organized because of the hints in this book. These lists and recommendations can be offered over a period of time. A brilliant prepping supply cache isn't always built overnight (even though it is able to be). Our recommendation is to start gradual and build up your substances through the years. Try to make it a habit to purchase a few objects each week. After a while, your prepper deliver package will develop. But don't experience overwhelmed if you're simply beginning or in case you're new to prepping. There are plenty of methods to grow your deliver cache even if you are on a decent price range.

Know How to Use Your Tools

We are going to endorse numerous tools and device in this ebook so one can increase the odds of your survival. Many preppers make the mistake of buying new equipment and testing them out for a couple of minutes and then storing them away. Take the time to test out and virtually get to know the way to use these tools. Practice cooking food, filtering water, and so on. When a disaster takes place you don't need to be getting to know as you cross.

Food Storage 101 – A Brief Overview

Before we dive into more advanced topics, we wanted to cover a short advent to meals garage for folks who are new to technique. Preparing a inventory of meals elements could be an crucial a part of your practise and survival. In times of crisis, disaster, or emergencies your food supply can be the lifeline that sustains you and your own family. Building up your meals supply can look like a daunting mission, however don't fear. Even if you begin preparing today and catastrophe strikes tomorrow you'll still be better off than hundreds of thousands of others.

Having an amazing food stock isn't just best for the apocalypse, but for any emergency. Every yr hurricanes, ice storms, earthquakes, wild fires, and different herbal disasters hit towns and houses leaving thousands unable to care for themselves. Having the assets to stay self enough in these times of disaster will provide you with a feeling of security, which is priceless in instances of turmoil when assist can be days away. It's never too overdue to begin preparing, and by using taking a few matters into consideration you'll be in your manner to having a strong deliver of meals very quickly.

When you're first beginning out on building your meals stock you want to construct slowly. Don't make the rash selection of going out and shopping for hundreds of kilos of complete grain wheat to store to your basement with the intention to likely cross horrific earlier than you're capable of use it. When you're accumulating components to your meals reserves you want to take into account to best buy what you'll use. If you're shopping for up resources which you recognise you and your family won't eat then you run the danger of taking an useless financial hit whilst the food expires. Start out small every week when you visit the grocery save and attempt handiest buying one or more gadgets of non-perishable meals. A few months of this and also you'll have a pleasant building up of food.

As your food garage expands you'll want to make certain to keep up a variety in your stock. Having variety for your weight loss program isn't simply important for bodily health, however mental fitness as properly. This may be mainly proper when you have youngsters. Feeding them the equal issue day by day might also cause them to lose their appetite, depleting them of the nutrients that they want to grow. Having a nicely rounded supply of canned items, dehydrated fruits and greens, smoked meats, goodies, and MREs can assist combat this monotony off.

Once you begin deciding on the types of foods you'll be storing you'll want to don't forget a few things. What does your finances appear to be? How many humans do I plan on feeding? How lengthy do I need my supply to last me? Answering these questions can help figure out whether or not you should spend money on MREs, or grocery sold canned items. If you're like most Americans on a budget then buying hundreds of packs of MREs to closing you for the subsequent three years is probably out of the question. However, having some packs in a computer virus out bag might be a terrific idea in case you want to get out in a hurry.

More than probable canned items, dehydrated end result and greens, and smoked meats will make up the majority of your supply. The reason I advise having "dehydrated" end result and veggies and "smoked" meats is that you may now not have the ability to refrigerate. You'll additionally want to supplement your food stock with vitamins and minerals, which require no refrigeration either. Most diet supplements have a shelf life of years, but you're still capable of eat them after their expiration date. Like the whole lot else though they free their potency over time.

As your meals deliver grows so ought to the distance in which you shop it. The space need to be proportionate to the variety of human beings you may be feeding and the period of time you'll be feeding them. Every individual desires a certain quantity of caloric consumption to maintain a healthy weight and pastime stage. Let's say the average character for your institution needs thousand calories to sustain themselves in step with day. If you're going to have 5 humans on your organization with a six month supply of food, then that means you're going to need to have space to shop 1.Eight million energy. Now, that range appears lofty, however you get the factor I'm looking to make. Be sure to have enough meals for the period of time you need to make yourself experience organized.

With the majority of society now not understanding how to nicely put together for disasters protective your food turns into increasingly critical as sources end up scarce. Keep locks on any food garage units which you have, and make sure it's concealed. If you are lucky enough so one can develop your personal food try hiding your end result and veggies among non-fit for human consumption plants. Most humans don't recognise how to become aware of which flowers are fit for human consumption and most effective a educated eye will be capable of find what they are able to devour out of your garden.

Everything has a shelf existence. With each passing day, week, and month that goes by the food that you have saved will begin to lose its nutritional potency. I might advise doing a weekly test of your supplies so you're continuously privy to what you have got to your reserves. You'll additionally need to do a more exact inspection each month or so to head over whatever which could have been disregarded for your weekly checks. During those inspections in case you're finding which you're throwing out massive amounts of meals that has expired, then you definitely'll recognise you're buying too much meals for the quantity of humans which you're feeding.

The ability to feed your self and your family throughout a time of hassle is a essential pillar to your survival. Through planning and vigilance you'll be capable of maintain a degree of health that others can't. The worst factor that could show up is not being organized whilst catastrophe strikes, and then being a part of the horde of millions of folks who are looting and rummaging thru shops to grab their palms on anything they could locate. Don't be a part of the problem. Be a part of the answer.

10 meals storage Mistakes to Avoid

The recommendation we are going to offer you on this book has been gathered through interviewing and running with several preppers. These are all preppers that are ready for severa screw ups starting from natural to human-made failures. While we need you to achieve success as possible to your food garage prepping, we are going to check the top 10 mistakes preppers make. By expertise those flaws you may keep away from these pitfalls accordingly you may be that much more successful. So permit's take a look at the pinnacle 10 mistakes preppers make while starting their meals supply.

Make Sure To Actually Use Your Storage

The first mistake that we are going to talk about is the failure to without a doubt cook and use your food garage in ordinary existence. Many preppers make the error of stockpiling the essential items most effective to preserve them locked in storage. They feel that they have got checked off the container for meals garage and they can move directly to the following region of prepping. This is a big mistake and may lead to troubles if a disaster does occur.

Cooking Prepper Meals Is any other Skill

First off, cooking with dehydrated and freeze dried items is a whole lot distinct than cooking with fresh items. It can be hard, and creating food that flavor nicely may be quite difficult if you are inexperienced. We rather recommend buying a prepper cookbook or search on line for meals that you can practice cooking with. Just like everyday food, you need to exercise cooking your prepper food. Try to prepare dinner one prepper meal every week so that you can practice and hone your competencies.

Taste

Many prepper food gadgets taste significantly one-of-a-kind than their sparkling opposite numbers. Some taste precisely the same. But you need to always check every meal and spot how your circle of relatives reacts. Once a catastrophe does occur you don't want to surprise your family with meals that are not great to your flavor buds. This is why we advise starting sluggish and planning your prepper meals garage. Purchase more of the meals that your family enjoys while disposing of the food that are ugly.

Just because you are stocking up for a disaster doesn't suggest you can't enjoy the meals you cook. Keep in thoughts, a few prepper food gadgets are going to taste bland and absence flavor, however because of dietary records they could need to be kept round.

Mistakes

Many elements also are tough to cook with. These ingredients can be tough to combine and match or you could find that they observe to only a few food. You have to constantly try to hold staple meals items on your meals storage. These are items that can be used in a couple of food and elements that you're feeling comfortable cooking with. Remove any gadgets which you have tough cooking with or can only use on a few meals. Instead inventory up on staple gadgets and make sure you've got enough to cover your prepping dreams. All of those troubles may be avoided with the aid of truely using your stockpile and incorporating your food supply into your weekly meals.

Proper Containers

Another commonplace mistake we run across is using incorrect or no bins for storing food. The container, bag, or container that your food comes in is not acceptable storage until it especially is available in a container this is storage prepared. Many people will spend masses of greenbacks on meals items best to improperly store them. When a disaster does occur they quick find that their meals deliver is vain as the meals has spoiled or bugs have made their way into the deliver. This is a huge waste of cash and might dramatically lower your odds of survival.

Stacking Your Food Items

Another commonplace mistake that we see with inexperienced preppers is a failure to properly stack and stable their food supply. We understand that it is able to be tough to find space to save all your survival food however please makes certain your meals is nicely secured. There are numerous cases of earthquakes, tornadoes, and hurricanes shaking prepper's houses and pulling down shelves of garage meals. This can destroy mason jars, rip bags, and knock the pinnacle off cans and jars. Please make sure you secure your meals supply and use the right bins which can be constructed to face up to a piece of harm. Nothing is greater disheartening then surviving a catastrophe handiest to comprehend you have got misplaced your entire meals supply.

Diversification and Balance

Failure to nicely diversify and stability your food stockpile is some other common mistake we see with new preppers. They will stockpile positive substances which includes wheat, dehydrated items, or freeze dried items. The trouble with buying these objects in bulk with out thinking about the meals you'll cook is that maximum instances you may be left with an abundance of 1 item and shortage of every other. This is why we suggest you begin sluggish and check earlier than scaling up. This will come up with a feel of which items you need and what sort of of every item you require. Just making big shopping of 1 object at a time will cause pointless quantity of sure objects being bought. This can soak up critical area to your meals garage areas and cost you pointless amounts of cash.

The Importance of Quick Meals

Many preppers will stockpile numerous amounts of components and create a big meals deliver handiest to comprehend that the majority in their meals require quite a few cooking. When you are attempting to live to tell the tale a catastrophe cooking can take in valuable time. Never underestimate the strength of MREs or items that can be speedy consumed without any practise. After a long day of labor, a quick meal may be vital on your fulfillment. Small meals that are easy to prepare are also essential for a computer virus-out situation. We want you to have your own malicious program-out-bag with meals already prepared. Having those objects available can assist you to bring those quick meals with you if you have the time and area to hold them.

Sweets and Other Morale Boosting Foods

Other areas that a few preppers neglect to stockpile are chocolates and physiological foods. Many preppers will attention on stockpiling simplest foods that especially dietary. This is vital and you need to usually look for ingredients which can be nutrient wealthy and provide power. But the importance of small candies, sugar ingredients, and other comfort meals have to not be left out. Many prepping foods do now not flavor very good and are designed to make sure your survival. This can decrease morale in particular if you have small children. Small chocolates and ethical boosting foods which might be smooth to keep ought to always be blanketed for your meals deliver. These can convey comfort to each kids and adults regardless of how hard the scenario you are in.

Creating a Supply of Vitamins

We are always going to suggest you pay close interest to the dietary values of all of the meals which you stockpile. You need to ensure which you and your circle of relatives are receiving enough nutrients to fight off disorder and continue to be wholesome. Sometimes, especially while your meals supply is dwindling and also you need to begin rationing; you may be vulnerable to diet depletion. This is why we tremendously recommend that you put money into nutrients similarly to the opposite gadgets for your meals supply. Having nutrients available will allow piece of mind that your family is receiving their proper nutrients even in case you meals deliver is dwindling.

Variety

Variety is important for long term survival. Eating the same food day in and day trip can turn out to be unbearable. The closing mistake we're going to speak about is ensuring you diversify and upload range on your meals garage supply. Most failures will final for just a few days or perhaps weeks but that doesn't suggest you shouldn't put together for huge scale screw ups. Large scale disasters can final months and you need to make certain you have sufficient food and that your meals has enough range to final. Don't get stuck repeating the same food day in and time out. This is simply some other cause we need you to rotate your food supply into regular cooking. This will assist you to enlarge and exercise new food which make certain which you are adding range on your food supply.

Make Sure You Include Vinegar

Vinegar may be a remarkable addition for your survival repertoire. This surprise liquid is a wonderful all round device for cleaning, cooking, and disinfecting. All of those makes use of, coupled with its cheap charge tag and long shelf existence, can be a treasured asset for you and your survival in a disaster. Today we willtake a have a look at how vinegar's ordinary makes use of can further enhance your first-class of dwelling after the sirens wail.

Disinfectant

Infection and sickness are going to be two of your worst enemies in a world wherein contemporary clinical packages might not be available. Disinfecting your food prepping and sanitation areas might be critical. With the quantity of human germs and dirt building up that those two regions stumble upon there can be a whole lot of possibilities for ailment to spread. Cleaning the ones regions with vinegar will give you an part in fighting the undesirable stumbling blocks of infection. Lack of proper hygiene, bad sanitation conduct, insufficient amounts of water, and lowered immune systems because of loss of vitamins can all cause a disastrous scenario. Vinegar's potential to combat off bacteria can dramatically boom your survival odds whilst implemented in your day by day recurring.

Clean Water Filters

Water filtration could be an important aspect of your survival. If you're using water filters to help you create drinkable water from ponds, lakes, or rivers, then you'll need which will deliver them a proper cleansing to boom their sturdiness. One trouble with water filters that we have a tendency to overlook is how hard it may be to certainly easy them. If you have got a huge organization of humans you're going to need to supply them with enough clean water to live to tell the tale. With hundreds of gallons of water being pumped into your filters you're going to have a build up of grime, mold, and mildew. This buildup can result in inefficient pumps and a lack of proper filtration. Soaking the elements in vinegar will remove this building up and increase the performance and durability of your water filters.

Window Frost

If you're in a place where there's the possibility for frost for the duration of the wintry weather seasons then vinegar canhelp prevent your windows from frosting over. Mixing water with vinegar in a spray bottle allow you to defrost your vehicle windows to permit for a clean subject of imaginative and prescient. Being able to see what's coming is a life saving asset in case you're pressured to evacuate quick. Using vinegar in the windows of your own home will also have the same impact. Having a clear view of sight from your property allow you to detect and neutralize for home invasions.

Increase the Life of Propane Wicks

If you're the use of propane as a sustainable fuel supply for yourself then vinegar can growth the life span of the wicks in your propane lanterns. Soaking your wicks in vinegar will permit your wicks to burn longer, to be able to are available in on hand for pro-longed crisis conditions. This is a small detail, but each danger to maximize your performance in a survival state of affairs will increase your hazard of creating it out alive.

Natural Air Freshener

When you're in a situation with a large number of survivors who may additionally lack the sources to keep a healthful hygiene stage, or proper sanitation efforts, the scent of bacteria and feces can end up in problem. While the odor of vinegar may be potent it will help neutralize the opposite smells in your location. If you're going to be held desk bound in one region for an prolonged time frame then you definately're going to need to simply accept the fact of how rancid a collection of human beings can get while restrained to close quarters. Vinegar let you face that fact and convey a degree of civility into your situation.

Mildew and Mold

Buildups of mold and mould can also be unsafe in your health if you're living in a cramped environment. The loss of mild and right cooling can make your survival vicinity a breeding floor for all types of mould. A habitual wipe down with vinegar for your showering stations can prevent, and fast kill, mould and mildew.

Natural Preservative

Whether you're developing your personal fruits and vegetables, or have a preceding stock pile, coating them in vinegar can help increase their shelf existence. Vinegar prevents rotting which should buy you time if you're going to can or dehydrate your food. This is an in particular beneficial tip in case you are collecting a massive harvest or foraging for food.

Pickled Eggs

If you're going to be pickling eggs vinegar is an important ingredient in this manner. Pickled eggs aren't handiest precious assets of protein and energy, but they final for a completely long time.

Sooth burns and heal cuts

Cuts, bruises, and burns are all injuries you may come upon all through your survival. Making positive these accidents don't increase to infections is crucial. Remember, your immune system may be depleted because of insufficient energy and the majority of your strength will be diverted to duties apart from cleaning, which can result in an growth in micro organism to creep into those wounds. Even small cuts and injuries can quick cause huge time hassle.

Clean Grills and Cooking Equipment

When water is in brief deliver and also you need to efficaciously smooth your grill or cooking equipment vinegar may be a dependable replacement. Wiping down these stations will let you reduce via the grime and grease increase.

How to Store Your Food Supply

Properly storing your meals deliver in the best packing containers is crucial in case you are going keep away from meals spoilage. Knowing which field to use for positive meals is a huge a part of know-how and implementing proper food garage. Remember nothing is worse than catastrophe happening as you realise that your meals supply has been infected. Lucky for you, there are various one-of-a-kind food storage boxes on the market that will help you preserve your meals supply for lengthy periods of time. Let's test the subsequent meals garage bins you could use:

Vacuum Sealed Bags

A vacuum sealer and vacuum sealed luggage are important elements for lengthy-time period meals garage. Vacuum sealed baggage are not best extremely versatile, but they are able to preserve meals for a wonderful deal of time. We noticeably endorse you invest in a pinnacle-notch vacuum sealer and Mylar luggage.

Mylar vs. Plastic Bags

The first step in the vaccine sealing method is to buy Mylar baggage and oxygen absorbers. Do not use the clear plastic baggage that include your vacuum sealer. Not handiest are these clear plastic baggage very thin, however additionally they allow light to permeate the surface. Mylar baggage are thick and remaining lots longer than their clean counterparts. Oxygen absorbers are also essential to feature for your Mylar bags to keep away from oxygenation and keep the meals for longer durations of time. Numerous one of a kind forms of meals may be preserved with Mylar bags and a vacuum sealer. This manner may be sluggish before everything, but with a bit practice it gets easier.

Food Grade Buckets

Food grade buckets offer you the option to store big amounts of food. Food grade buckets aren't simplest very clean to stack but are extremely flexible. We advocate that you store all of your Mylar bags in food grade buckets as that is a effective one- mixture. Food grade buckets are tremendous for stacking, averting the enemies of meals garage, and can be used for severa different activities as well.

Gamma Lids vs. Regular Lids

You have alternatives to seal your buckets: Gamma lids and everyday meals storage lids. Gamma lids will maintain your buckets air tight, that's vital for meals that can destroy from contact with air. Regular covers will paintings properly with ingredients that are already packaged and you simply need the versatility of the bucket for garage. When doubtful, go along with a Gamma lid.

#10 Cans

#10 cans are the aluminum cans that can keep whatever from beans to freeze-dried foods. You can buy these cans and upload them to your food supply. These cans are smaller than a 5 gallon meals bucket which makes them critical for storing in smaller regions. The downside to #10 cans is they can be difficult to buy in bulk except you leave near a cannery or a Mormon Church.

Mason Jars

Mason jars are every other brilliant food storage object that you ought to take advantage of. Vacuum sealers are to be had for mason jars and it's pretty easy to discover ways to shop and vacuum seal those jars. Mason jars are smaller than the other food storage objects that we stated above which makes them awesome to keep in small, inconspicuous places. Make certain your mason jars are properly secured as they're made from glass and may be pretty fragile.

Pouches, Bags, and Other Storage Items

There are numerous different meals storage gadgets inclusive of resalable luggage, pouches, and containers that you can use to construct your meals storage deliver. Many times, pre-packaged survival meals and substances will come with their very own pouch or bag. When the usage of these pre-made objects ensure which you read the instructions cautiously. Some will want oxygen absorbers and you will want to reseal them with a vacuum sealer once they're opened. Take the 10 minutes to read and apprehend the commands or you can waste a whole bag of survival meals.

Extending The Shelf Life Of Your Food

Extending the shelf existence of your meals to final you for weeks, months, or maybe years at a time can look like a frightening task. We'll cross over some matters that you can do to assist maximize the shelf-life and performance of your food. With all the time you spend amassing and building up your meals inventory there must be same care in the amount of time and preparation that you deliver to keeping your food.

Increasing the shelf existence of your food assist you to cut down for your waste. The average American household throws away twenty-five percent of their bought meals. That's a rate tag ranging everywhere from $1,365 to $2,275 in step with yr. These financial resources that you'll store may be placed towards different substances that you'll want. Imagine the kind of generator you'll have the ability to shop for to maintain your home running at some stage in a energy outage with that type of money.

Preserving your food not most effective adds dollars to your bank account, but it is able to add years on your lifestyles. Keeping your meals sparkling for longer durations of time permits you to get the most out of the nutrients your meals offers. The common person doesn't get the right amount of vitamins on a day by day basis to stay healthy. This can be compounded exponentially in a survival situation. The freshness of you meals will assist you combat those factors so that you can preserve a suit body during times of pressure.

The first belongings you'll need to take a look at to help lengthen the shelf life of your food are the boxes you have. The cloth the box is manufactured from can play an critical function in how lengthy your meals stays sparkling. Glass jars can be useful packing containers as they let you see their contents without problems, they're inexpensive, reusable, and may come up with an air tight seal. The downside to glass jars is that they may be fragile and aren't the maximum green space savers. Tupperware and different plastic packing containers permit for less difficult garage use, however have the capacity to wear faster as time passes.

Taking a take a look at the substances to your foods allow you to decide how long they're going to remaining. This may match with out saying, however meals with preservatives will ultimate longer than foods with out them. Sugar and positive acidic components are natural preservatives that could help amplify your meals's lifespan. Organic products that bolster the reality that they don't have any preservatives will go to pot faster. The advertising and demand for those organic products have additionally made them more pricey to purchase, so via ignoring them you'll be saving money.

A mixture of warmth, cold, air, light, moisture, smells, and pests can purpose your meals to destroy. You'll want to consider the type of meals which you have and the quality method to save it so it retains its freshness. Vegetables like garlic, onions, and shallots must be saved in cool, dry places. Dry items, nuts, and spices may be saved in cabinets to assist keep away from publicity to mild and humidity as a way to be your important enemies.

If you need to take the shelf lifestyles of your end result and vegetable even further you may dehydrate them to help boom the lifespan in their nutrients. You can buy a dehydrator everywhere from fifty to 2 hundred bucks. The method of dehydrating your fruits and vegetables can take eight to twelve hours, but the owner's guide of your dehydrator may be able to offer you with the specifics needed to use it properly. The huge things to take into account while getting ready foods to be dehydrated are to ensure that you're using wholesome, ripe ingredients and make sure to reduce them proportionally to make sure even drying.

When it comes to meats the satisfactory upkeep can be freezing them, however in case you don't have get admission to to a generator to gasoline your freezer then smoking meats can be a great alternative to expanding their shelf lifestyles. Smoking can be accomplished with whatever. It may be a hollow in the floor, or a multi thousand greenback smoker. Whatever you operate you'll need to make sure that the meat stays a hundred and eighty-225 tiers. This is called hot smoking and it cooks the meals even as additionally including taste. For each 12 hours you smoke your meat it will closing for about every week.

You can also treatment your meat to extend its shelf lifestyles. This can be a more viable option for you in case you don't have the time or resources to smoke your meat. When you're curing your meats you'll need to ensure you've got components: curing salts and sodium nitrates. The sodium nitrates used in curing assist combat the bacteria botulism, which could result in paralysis and motive respiration issues. However, you don't need to add an excessive amount of sodium nitrates to your meats as excessive doses can be poisonous. Use the ten:ninety ratio as an amazing rule of thumb for a sodium nitrate to curing salt usage.

Taking the time and precautions to maximize your meals's capacity is some thing anyone should do. We stay in a world of finite assets and with the amount of waste that maximum human beings produce in recent times those resources are going to run out speedy. If all of us take the stairs to maximize our resources to prepare for this truth, then we ought to potentially save you some of the disasters that we're preparing for. Now, that's what I call being part of the solution.

List of Foods You Should Stockpile

The following is the listing you have to don't forget when beginning your food deliver. Remember it all starts with a plan so make certain you're recording your meals. This list is made out of foods and gadgets that speedy disappear as soon as a catastrophe moves. These are excessive demand ingredients and having a geared up stockpile with these items dramatically increases your odds for survival need to a catastrophe arise.

Water Is Still #1

You constantly need to make sure you have the right quantity of water to be had to you at all times. These objects are very important however please do now not neglect your water supply. Many preppers underestimate the amount of water they want to survive for an extended time frame. We will cover your water supply and a way to nicely shop water in a while in this e book but you ought to continually don't forget that water is primary.

Appetite Fatigue and How to Fight It

Before we begin on list meals which you should be stockpiling, we want to cowl urge for food fatigue. Appetite fatigue refers to the issues with consuming comparable food day in and time out. This phenomenon occurs in general with human beings in the military who devour similar MREs every day. Often instances they'll lose their urge for food and must force meals into their our bodies. This can lead to a loss of right nutrients, lack of judgment, and signs of starvation. Let's take a look at one-of-a-kind ways you could fight appetite fatigue.

Comfort meals

We noted in advance the significance of getting some consolation foods in your stockpile. While those ingredients may not be the healthiest or offer the most dietary cost they will offer you with a psychological improve. Sugars or sweet tasting foods combined with dietary survival foods let you keep away from appetite fatigue.

Spices

Many meals, specially freeze-dried and dehydrated, lack flavor. Spices are a top notch manner to add some taste to these food. Spices are very smooth to save and sure spices have medicinal use similarly to supporting you fight off appetite fatigue. We pretty endorse you spend a while and upload your preferred spices to your food supply.

Canned Liquids

You can kill two birds with one stone with canned liquids. Not best will these foods offer you with critical re-hydration, however they may also offer you with essential vitamins. We endorse you focus your interest on coconut milk, evaporate milk, pineapple juice, and condensed milk. You can also use plenty of these drinks to assist cook or upload flavor in your food.

Dehydrated and Canned Meats

Meats will provide you with the vital protein and energy you want to live to tell the tale. Protein is critical while you are attempting to live to tell the tale a disaster, and failure to have a right deliver of meat can decrease your odds of survival dramatically. We suggest purchasing jerky, tuna, and different resources of dehydrated and canned meats. Easy-to-keep meats now not handiest flavor excellent, but may be literally be a existence saver.

Coffee and Tea

Two items that many preppers leave off their list of objects to stockpile are espresso and tea. Coffee and teas are very cheaper and may be blended with water to make a tasty drink. Not only will they rehydrate you but the caffeine will offer you with a lift of strength. This is crucial if you are working the night shift or you've got the night time watch in a disaster state of affairs. Due to a loss of proper vitamins many human beings will sense exhausted when looking to survive a disaster. A short caffeine boost will allow you to get the work accomplished you want to live to tell the tale.

Protein Bars

We cited above the importance of protein in the course of a disaster conditions. Not handiest are protein bars a splendid source of power and protein, but they require no practise at all. They are clean to p.C. And are essential if you're going to explore and need to leave home base. Many protein bars are also full of sugars which lead them to a remarkable comfort meals. Protein bars also are surprisingly less expensive and you can purchase them in bulk. They are also extraordinarily clean to keep and have a very lengthy shelf lifestyles.

Whole Wheat Flour

Whole wheat flour is critical for making numerous one-of-a-kind meals objects. Whole wheat flour has greater nutrients than its white wheat counterpart which is why we endorse it. It can be bought in bulk quantities, however make certain you take a look at it before you buy large portions. The distinction among white and wheat flour can make certain meals flavor distinct. But entire wheat flour is important to any prepper's food garage stockpile.

Corn

Your meals deliver need to have an abundance of corn. Not simplest is corn smooth to store it's also very inexpensive. You need to have huge quantities of corn as a grain and additionally corn that has been canned or either dehydrated or freeze dried. This permits you a piece of variety while you are planning out your food storage.

Sugar

Sugar is every other object that may be purchased in bulk and is vital in preventing off urge for food fatigue. Sugar has lengthy shelf life and is very clean to shop. There are severa cooking uses for sugar and it's very less expensive.

Honey

Honey is any other comfort food item that can be used while making numerous varieties of food. Organic honey is also very nutritional and has the capacity to spike your blood sugar with a purpose to give you a lift of energy. This is one motive that honey is popular as an additive on your prepper breakfast. Honey is also very clean to store and has a long shelf existence.

Pre-Packaged Foods

There also are numerous prepackaged ingredients which have an extended shelf life. These meals are perfect as they are able to speedy be organized by means of each person to your own family. These food also are considered consolation foods as they could trigger recollections of existence before a disaster. Examples consist of ramen and mac and cheese.

Vinegar

Vinegar is likewise important in severa cooking activities in addition to medicinal purposes. Vinegar is a herbal anti-septic which may be used to deal with wounds and disinfect surfaces. One trouble that many preppers face is disease and sickness. When you're jogging on caloric deficit, your immune machine will now not be a robust. You want to pay greater interest to disinfecting surfaces and making sure your own family is safe from germs and bacteria.

Drink Mixes

Prepackaged Gatorade, Kool-Aid, hot cocoa, and tea are all a top notch way to add flavor on your water. These are another time essential for your survival and are tremendous for restoring consolation. These drink mixes are also vital in case you need to drink filtered water which may have an unpleasant flavor. These drink mixes can masks the flavor and will let you get the hydration you and your own family wishes.

Dehydrated Eggs

Eggs are first-rate supply of protein and are especially endorsed to be protected for your meals supply. Eggs can be utilized in quite a few one of a kind food and are pretty versatile. They also are wholesome sources of protein and fat.

Canned Meals

Canned meals which includes chili, soups, and stews also are to be protected for your food supply. These cans are very clean to save and stockpile and feature a completely long shelf existence. They are also very easy to put together and require very little effort. Canned food are also critical in case you are at the flow and decide to bug-out and evacuate from your house.

Waxing Cheese

Waxing cheese can be hard to locate however having cheese to your food deliver ought to be something that you try for. Waxing cheese is ordinary cheese this is blanketed by a layer of wax. This prevents mold from developing at the cheese and extends its shelf existence.

Sauce, Sauce, Sauce

Another wonderful manner to speedy upload taste or masks bland tasting ingredients is with extraordinary sauces. Numerous special kinds of tomato or other sauces can add range to any meal. Sauces are extremely easy to store and we especially advise which you stockpile your favored ones.

Rice

Rice is extraordinarily reasonably-priced and can provide your own family nutrients to survive. Rice is extraordinarily versatile and may be utilized in severa food. Rice is also a terrific aspect dish or compliment to a prime course. Easy to prepare and eat, rice may be cooked quick either in your own home or on the road. These are just a few reasons why rice is a prepper's nice friend.

Canned Vegetables and Fruit

We additionally relatively advocate you stock up on canned veggies and fruit. This ought to be a no-brainer and you must always have an extra deliver of these two. Once again, cans are extremely flexible and have to be utilized in severa disaster conditions. Look to buy those items in bulk or store coupons and you could locate some brilliant discounts in case you pay close attention to nearby sales.

Cornmeal and Oats

Cornmeal and oats are also treasured resources of protein. They also are quite flexible and numerous food may be cooked and created by way of the usage of these two. They have lengthy shelf lives and can be purchased in bulk. Make them a concern in case you're going to begin your prepper meals deliver.

Peanut Butter

Peanut butter is another exceptional food which you should keep to your meals cache. Not only does peanut butter taste extraordinary, but it's very nutrition. Peanut butter will give you the strength you need to tackle the day and ensure which you survive. We distinctly propose eating peanut butter as a morning snack and during the day while you feel hungry or worn-out.

Jams and Jellies are some other supply of sugar which can add variety and taste for your food. You can purchase jams in small bins commonly from eating place supply shops. These small packages have a long shelf lifestyles and can be without problems stored away.

Cooking Oils

Always keep in mind to hold a inventory of cooking oils. Many preppers will spend all their time stocking up on food gadgets however neglect cooking oils. Coconut oil has a shelf existence of round 2 years and have to be used in place of olive oil. Creamery butter also can be used and might remaining for 2-3 years.

Canned and Dehydrated Fish

Tuna is a first rate source of protein and has a totally lengthy shelf lifestyles. Be cautious with how many cans of tuna you consume as tuna is a high source of mercury. Make certain you spread out the amount of tuna over a period of days and you will be first-class.

Potato Flour

If you've got gluten allergies or you've got family individuals that have gluten intolerance, you ought to add potato flour in your food stockpile. You could make numerous foods with potato flour and it is able to be a amazing replacement for ordinary flour. We enormously advocate that you inventory up on potato flour similarly to your flour supply.

Crackers

Crackers are some other object that have a long shelf life and might provide you with numerous options for meals. While they've little dietary advantages you can upload them to most meals. Spreading jams or peanut butter on crackers may be a awesome manner to make a brief meal. You can purchase some brands of crackers in #10 cans which notably extends their shelf-lifestyles.

Pasta

Since pasta has little to no moisture or fats content it has a completely lengthy shelf existence. Pasta is likewise extraordinarily versatile and can be used in numerous survival conditions. Pasta is also very inexpensive and most supermarkets and grocery stores will constantly have deals on containers of pasta.

Beans

Beans produce an notable amount of calories consistent with pound and have to be a staple item in your food deliver. Beans will offer you with the essential power to survive. They also are a remarkable source of fiber which is extraordinarily essential especially while you are not on a everyday weight loss program. We suggest stocking up on all forms of beans and making sure you've got a extensive variety at your disposal.

Dried Fruits

Dried ingredients are complete of nutrients and also can be ate up at the pass. Raisins and other dried end result are vital for survival. Remember that there's a difference among dried and dehydrated so you want to make sure that you're rotating your dried culmination. They will not have the identical shelf existence as your other dehydrated or freeze-dried foods.

Iodized Salt

Salt is some other important item that you ought to consist of in your prepper pantry. If you appearance lower back in history you may find that salt turned into a huge commodity. Well, in a survival situation salts price skyrockets. You need to ensure you've got enough to continue to exist the duration of the disaster. Salt can offer treasured nutrients that your body needs to stay healthy, kill bacteria, treat wounds, and additionally maintain food. We particularly advocate you make a bulk purchase of salt and ensure you have got sufficient to your prepper pantry.

Nuts

Another outstanding source of protein are nuts. Nuts are short, smooth, and may be used as terrific travel food. They are a super source of severa nutrients and we distinctly propose that you have nuts accessible. Easy to eat, they're additionally considered a consolation meals that may be utilized in severa other meals.

Herbs and Spices

We noted in the starting of this bankruptcy the importance of heading off appetite fatigue. The satisfactory way to keep away from this trouble is through the usage of herbs and spices to feature taste to your food. Herbs and spices have a long shelf existence and can be very clean to shop. We suggest you look into purple pepper, dill, cumin, rosemary, and saffron.

Vodka

Vodka has numerous uses and is quite versatile. Besides drinking vodka, you may prepare dinner with vodka and also use vodka for medicinal functions. Many people also overlook the significance of bartering in a survival state of affairs. Vodka may be a top barter object and might command pretty a charge. Vodka is a exceptional disinfectant and may be used to deal with severa wounds and sores.

Baking Soda and Baking Powder

Don't forget to feature baking soda and baking powder for your prepper stockpile. Both are crucial for cooking and allowing your baked goods to upward push. Both baking powder and baking powder are vital for cooking and ought to be a staple item to your survival cache.

Yeast

Yeast is another element this is important for cooking in a survival scenario. The trouble with yeast is that it has a very short shelf existence of only a few months. With that being stated, you want to consciousness and rotate out your yeast on a persistent foundation.

Chocolate

Chocolate should be included in your prepper deliver cache for severa reasons. First, it's a comfort food this is complete of anti-oxidants. Chocolate can deliver you with a short power enhance and it also enables combat off starvation. Chocolate need to be turned around together with your fashionable weekly meals.

Condiments

Condiments are clean to save and crucial to help fight off food fatigue. Most condiments have an extended shelf existence and can be purchased in bulk at most restaurant supply stores. We extraordinarily suggest searching into condiments and including them in your food supply.

In-Depth Look at Your Food Supply

Purchasing and stockpiling food components, within the event of a disaster, is a tactic that everybody must adhere to. Having a backup supply of food is essential in any disaster and will dramatically growth your odds of survival. When a disaster occurs, your nearby grocery shops will straight away run out of food supplies or meals will quick be looted and stolen. If there's a energy outage, commonplace everyday ingredients that need to be kept cool will quick disappear. Without a proper food supply, you will discover your self venturing from your safe residence looking for meals sources. Leaving your secure residence to are seeking for meals places you in risk and also exposes your property to looters. If you start to run on a caloric deficit your energy stage will gradual and your decision making will even end up cloudy. Government resource and supplies should also not matter on and might depart you ready weeks for meals. These elements can also be rationed off simplest leaving you with the naked minimum food and water intake. In this bankruptcy we can talk approaches to well shop, select, and create your meals stockpiles.

Food Storage Enemies

Maintaining the best and preserving your meals source should be your top precedence in terms of developing a food supply. Nothing is extra risky than a disaster going on and understanding that your meals supply has been infected. In order to preserve your meals preserved you have to keep away from the following enemies:

Heat

Heat will dramatically decrease the shelf life of your meals deliver. You meals ought to be in cool area, that is most effective climate managed. A small air con unit is probably a smart investment if you are building a massive food deliver room.

Air

Exposure to air can also dramatically lessen the shelf life of your food deliver. You need to make certain which you are acquainted with vacuum sealing in case you are going to properly keep your food. Investing in oxygen absorbers may also permit you to get rid of any oxygen that would contaminate your meals deliver.

Light

Light is every other enemy of your food supply. Light will no longer only lower the shelf-existence of your food, but it will additionally increase the heat on your room. Make sure your meals is saved in a darkish location.

Humidity and Moisture

Moisture and humidity are also known to lower the shelf-lifestyles of your meals supply. Make certain your food is kept in a cool and dry place. Look to put money into dehumidifier and moisture manipulate equipment.

Expiration Dates

Even even though you're saving up meals to your emergency deliver, you need to make sure you rotate. Many styles of meals have expiration dates which you need to be aware about. Rotating your meals is the fine approach to clear up this hassle. Your food garage deliver must be used and eaten to avoid meals hitting the expiration mark.

Pests

The last enemy of your food deliver that we're going to speak about is pests. There are many different sorts of family pests which can chew thru and contaminate your food supply. You need to actively screen your food deliver for any pest improvement and take the proper steps to repair the problem must it rise up.

Protecting your food from pests

When harboring large quantities of food you're certain to attract a few unwanted pests. These pests have the potential to wreak havoc on your food supply. While none of your substances will final for all time taking the precautions to protect your meals can assist extend their lifespan. Let's move over a few arrangements you may do to assist save you your meals inventory from being infiltrated by way of unwanted pests.

Having strong, durable packing containers will act as a first line of protection. Mylar bags and buckets with gamma seal lids are an excellent start. The mylar bags have a constructed in layer of protection that enables prevent moisture, which cuts down at the increase and build up of mold. The gamma seal lids are incredible for containers which you constantly want to re-open and seal to get entry to meals. These lids create an airtight and leak-proof seal to help preserve the meals inner clean, and preserve bugs out.

Identifying the sorts of pests which are compromising your food also can be beneficial. Common pests that sneak into food components are flour beetles, noticed-toothed grain beetles, and carpet beetles. Once you've diagnosed the kind of bug you're coping with the next factor you'll need to recall is the level of infestation for your meals, and from there you can determine whether or not it's far salvageable or no longer. If you're managing a very moderate infestation, then freezing the meals will kill the pests. You need to stash the meals in a deep freeze for 3 to four days to make certain you're killing the pests in all ranges in their lifestyles cycle. Some humans would suggest the use of pesticides, but I could keep away from the use of dangerous chemical compounds to treat the food considering the fact that that is what you'll be putting in you and your family's bodies for consumption. If the contamination is past the brink of seeking to store it, then you definitely'll need to discard that fabric as fast as possible to prevent it from spreading to different food components.

If you're looking for a safe and effective method of pest control this is an alternative to harmful pesticides, then traps baited with pheromones, which might be non-poisonous chemical compounds that trap pests into them, might be an excellent area to start. Gemplers.Com is a exquisite resource for this form of pest manipulate. They provide numerous merchandise that can help you not only with protective your food garage, but also any plants you grow.

Another preventative measure of preserving pests out is to make sure you're inspecting your substances on a ordinary basis. Keep an stock of all your objects, when you bought them, and their shelf existence. This will help you stay prepared, and if you do a weekly inspection you'll understand exactly what you have, and what you're going for walks low on, at any given time. In addition to the weekly assessments you'll want to do a completely distinct inspection of your substances every month looking for strains of pests, or different sources of infection that could ruin your meals garage.

When you're doing your weekly inspection of your supplies you need to take that opportunity to make certain your meals garage region is clean. Wiping down containers, shelves, and flooring is an extremely smooth, and effective, preventative degree to help with pest control. Leaving spilled contents for your meals garage is an open invitation to any pest seeking out a loose meal.

Besides insects, the other pest a good way to go to pot your meals is oxygen. Leaving ingredients exposed and out within the open will boost up their decomposition. This is in which having solid containers will are available available. In addition to having a layer that protects in opposition to moisture the mylar baggage additionally prevent oxygen exposure. Oxygen absorber packs can be delivered to your components to growth your foods durability. In preceding troubles I've additionally stated using vacuum seal gadgets to help maintain meals sparkling longer.

Your packing containers, baggage, buckets, and lids should develop along with the dimensions of your meals supply. The variety of containers shouldn't completely out wide variety the amount of substances that you have, but it's always an awesome idea to preserve a few more empty containers accessible just in case. Adding in your supplies as you cross can even make it financially easier to prepare for emergencies.

As a long way because the specific varieties of manufacturers and fashions of garage containers that you may get I even have some other wonderful article in this difficulty wherein I'll dive into which bins come up with the most bang on your dollar.

Keeping an eye fixed on your meals garage must constantly be a concern. Whatever meals you have can be your lifeblood for an prolonged period of time and you need to make sure which you're looking after it. Remember to test your components for pests on a everyday basis and hold your food garage vicinity clean. Preparation must in no way start the next day. It starts nowadays.

Where Do You Store Your Food

The first idea which can come to thoughts whilst searching at our meals lists is, "Where am I going to keep all this food?" This is a exquisite point in particular in case you are having hassle locating area to your normal meals deliver. Many of these items can be hidden in one-of-a-kind rooms or areas and we definitely advocate that you have a couple of food deliver resources. You need to have one big food location this is in the advocate climate, however you may shop other ingredients that have longer shelf lives in distinct rooms. Spreading out your food supply rooms diversifies chance and will increase your odds of survival.

What Do You Store Your Food In

When you are storing your meals it's crucial to make certain that the meals is in the right boxes. Having your food in proper containers will dramatically boom its shelf life. We recommend that you begin investing in mason jars, food grade buckets, and gamma seal lids. Be cautious of domestic improvement buckets as they're no longer similar to meals grade buckets. Mylar luggage are also a notable way to maintain your food preserved and easy to save. Mason jars may be vacuum pressurized and Gamma seal lids will preserve your meals sealed close. #10 steel cans also are a high-quality way to shop your meals.

Start Small

If you are new to prepping and meals garage this could appear a bit overwhelming. The best advice we will give you is to begin small. Building a proper food supply for you and your own family can take months to properly build. We endorse that you begin small and actually start shopping for a few greater items at the grocery shop and including them to your food deliver each week. Picking some gadgets to double up on each week will slowly construct your food deliver supply and might not smash your budget at the equal time.

Rotate, Rotate, Rotate

Many people assume that your meals deliver is for emergency simplest and need to not be touched. This is a massive mistake and may cause meals being wasted because of expiration dates. Your food deliver must not be prevented as a substitute it should be circled. This way you are continuously the usage of your meals deliver every and every day. Just make sure that once you use one item you purchase a brand new one and "rotate" the brand new object to the lower back of the line. This will assist you to use the meals that close to expiration and maintain more energizing meals and materials prepared in case of an emergency.

Test, Test, Test

Many survival food kits are bought in large bulk orders to keep money. This can cause shopping food items that are not the great or taste that you desire. Dehydrated and frozen food elements also can flavor quite distinct than their fresh counterparts. You should always check out and buy small quantities of meals elements before making the jump with large purchases. Try out distinct recipes and food objects until you've got narrowed down your list to items your whole own family enjoys. Purchase a small sun heater and practice along with your circle of relatives cooking gadgets inside the again yard. This is a high-quality getting to know and bonding possibility in your circle of relatives. Most of the food objects we've got indexed are to be had in variety % or small starter kits.

Freeze Dried Vs. Dehydrated

When growing your food supply you are going to have different options to be had to you with reference to preserved food. We advocate which you try to hold each freeze-dried and dehydrated meals on your supply. Both have their execs and cons, but you should continually try every sort of food before creating a bulk purchase.

Freeze Dried Food

Freeze dried meals are usually extra costly than dehydrated foods. Freeze dried foods will allow you extra range for your alternatives with such favorites as ice cream sandwiches. Freeze dried ingredients are also very fragile and have a tendency to crumble. Freeze dried foods will last for 10+ years and most of the meals are tasty and quite fun. Freeze dried ingredients are not as nutritious as their counterpart. Freeze dried foods may also lose additional vitamins when they may be cooked.

Examples of Freeze Dried Foods:

Raspberries

Mandarin oranges

Pineapples

Corn

Red peppers

Green peppers

Mushrooms

Dehydrated Foods

Dehydrated foods are commonly inexpensive and less complicated to keep in comparison to freeze dried meals. You have a whole lot of options in relation to dehydrated ingredients a good way to permit you to prepare dinner different meals. Some dehydrated ingredients may also lack a few taste or may have a unique taste than you had been waiting for.

Examples of Dehydrated Foods:

Potatoes

Onions

Carrots

Sweet potatoes

Bananas

Hash browns

Green onions

Recommended Dehydrated Dairy:

Freeze-dried cheese

Milk

Butter

Eggs

What Should You Stockpile

Creating your meals deliver may be overwhelming and we urge you to start small. Start tracking your family's eating behavior and what sort of meals you devour in the course of a week. Take notes in your own family's preferred meals and see if you could reflect them in a survival situation. Easy meals that can be cooked at some stage in a survival state of affairs consist of:

Skillet food

Casseroles

Chili

Stews

Soups

You could be surprised at the number of dishes you can make with survival food. Recipes which can be high in canned foods, herb and spices, grains, rice, beans, dehydrated dairy, flour, sugar, and exclusive sauces can all be made from your survival deliver. Unfortunately, recipes that encompass bitter cream, cream cheese, huge quantities of dairy, positive veggies, and high protein resources may be difficult to save and create. Like we mentioned above, see if you may replica your own family's modern recipes and create them with preserved ingredients.

What to Consider

When creating your fundamental food stockpile you need to constantly keep some factors in thoughts. You need to make certain that you have a balanced series of massive meals that take time to prepare and smaller food that can be organized with little coaching. You need to also don't forget your garage location and the quantity of space you have got to be had. Large items inclusive of rice and grains will take in a number of area whilst cans and mason jars can be without problems stacked to save space. You need to additionally make sure you're aware about the nutritional price of all your resources. Having a food supply excessive in vitamins will make sure your health for the duration of survival durations. Also maintain in mind the shelf existence of the meals you're shopping and make sure you are well rotating your meals so as to avoid expiration. Lastly, your food supply ought to be complete of objects that quick run out within the first 48hrs during a disaster situation.

Looking At Disaster History

Taking a glance returned at prior failures permits us to create a fundamental meals deliver plan. By analyzing the meals items that promote out speedy all through catastrophe conditions, you can better prepare your food supply. When a disaster occurs these ingredients are long past from maximum stores within 24-48hrs and have to be blanketed on your food deliver:

Flour

Baking powder and baking soda

Sugar

Crackers

Honey

Spices

Dried fruits

Pickles

Nuts

Sports beverages

Olive oil

Whole grains

Cereal

Jerky

Popcorn

Salt

Pet foods

Canned end result

Soups

Rice

Pasta

Beans

Tomatoes

Canned vegetables

Canned meats

Tuna

Water

Protein drinks

Alcohol

Candy

Peanut butter

Tea

Salsa

Ramen noodles

Baby elements

Recommended Freeze Dried and Dehydrated Items:

Carrots

Jalapenos

Bananas

Hash browns

Onions

Potatoes

Raspberries

Oranges

Corn

Peppers

Mushrooms

Milk

Butter

Eggs

Cheese

Shortening powder

Cheese

Sour cream

Grapes

Sauces, Herbs, Spices

Pepper

Ginger

Mustard powered

Curry

Cinnamon

Chili powder

Cayenne pepper

Allspice

Diced garlic

Onion flakes

Table salt

Montreal steak sauce seasoning

Thyme

Tarragon

Sage

Rosemary

Oregano

Parsley

Mint

Dill

Chives

Bay leaves

Basil

Ranch dressing

Barbecue sauce

Mustard

Ketchup

A1 Steak Sauce

Worcester

Tabasco

Soy sauce

Basic Starter Kit

Creating exclusive recipes and looking to replicate your food can be a time consuming and lengthy procedure simply stocking up at the meals your family wants. If you're beginning and simply need the fundamentals we propose you start here:

2-4 containers of whey protein

1 gallon of olive oil

1 bag of oats

1 bag of salt

1 bag of sugar

1 bag of flour

2-4 large containers of sport drink mix

Ample amounts of Gatorade or other sports liquids

2 big jars of peanut butter

20 cans of meat (chicken, tuna, and so on.)

20 cans of greens

20 cans of fruit

15-20lbs of beans

10-20lbs of rice

This need to get you commenced at which point you may start to rotate and add in substances and other meals when you start to check them out and notice what recipes your circle of relatives likes.

No cooking No Problem

Foods that require little or no cooking are amazing for any catastrophe state of affairs. Make certain you stock up on:

Breakfast bars

"Just Add Water" or on the spot coffee

Pudding cups

Crackers

Cookies

Tuna cans

Candy

Rice cakes

Applesauce

Canned culmination

Jerky

Peanut butter

Cocoa blend

Sports drink blend

Protein powder

Canned pasta

V8 juice

Almonds

Energy bars

MREs

Basics You Should Consider Learning

You can improve the great of your own
food deliver through leaning a few keeping
strategies. Learning a way to jar one-of-a-
kind items is vital and will let you shop
your favourite recipes. Leaning a way to
bake your personal bread can even upload

range in your food supply. Lean dehydrating fundamentals and learn how to create and upload them on your meals deliver.

Water

During a disaster you furthermore may need to have an abundance of water. You cannot depend on your neighborhood shop for water during a catastrophe. Water is normally the primary item that is offered out throughout a disaster as most people handiest have a 48-72 hour supply of water. You need to take precautions and ensure that your own family has a supply of water and how to find other sources of water have to you run out. This bankruptcy might be devoted to helping you create your water deliver and we can additionally be discussing approaches to discover, clear out, and purify different assets of water.

Creating Your Water Supply

Just like your meals deliver, it is essential that you start stocking up on your water supply. FEMA recommends 2-3 weeks of water supply for your circle of relatives. As you would possibly have guessed, we endorse you prepare for an extended time line. As a rule of thumb, every member of your family have to be allotted two gallons of water an afternoon. One gallon for ingesting, and every other for cleaning, sanitation, and other makes use of. So take the quantity of your circle of relatives members and multiply by way of and then multiply by the number of days you want to survive and that must be your intention variety.

Where Do I Store All This Water?

When it involves storing water, we recommend a 3 tier gadget. This lets in you to maximise your water storage and makes positive that you have room for all the water your circle of relatives desires.

Tier 1

Tier one is made from water bottles and different small portable water containers. You can positioned these water bottles in any vicinity that isn't exposed to sunlight. This consists of closets, shelves, or under your bed. These water bottles are for quick get entry to and must be circled. You have to by no means save water that it's miles in plastic boxes for long intervals of time.

Tier 2

Tier 2 is created from large bottles of water or pallets of water. These boxes may be bought at bulk cut price chains including Costco. Buying in bulk with coupons or watching for deals is the quality manner to buy tier 2 waters if you're on a finances.

Tier 3

Tier three is your huge water box that is supposed to store massive amounts of water. This quantity of water goes to big and immobile. This water tank can be saved indoors or out.

Other Sources of Water

You want to ensure which you have sufficient water for an prolonged time frame however what happens in case you want to find different assets of water? Understanding in which to locate extra water sources and the way to filter out and purify water can dramatically boom your odds of survival. This ability is vital in particular if you have evacuated and you can't rely upon your water supply at your secure house.

Purifying, Filtering, and Treating Water

When locating a new water supply, it's far imperative which you take the proper course of action to clear out and purify that water source. Drinking contaminated or poisonous water could be your remaining pass. Always continue with intense warning while ingesting any sort of water. Seeking out extra water assets should continually be your closing hotel.

Be Aware Of Chemicals

The following filters and purification methods will best work on water that is chemical free. Purifying and filtering water that is contaminated with chemicals will no longer work. You want to be aware about the water supply you are deciding on and you need to make certain there's no chemical infection. If you have any doubts approximately chemical compounds inside the water or within the area, do no longer drink the water and flow on to some other supply.

Use a Coffee Filter

We are going to endorse coffee filters in both your deliver kits and your bug-out-bags. Coffee filters are exceptional for filtering out water earlier than you purify it. Coffee filters will acquire maximum of the dirt, debris, and sediment earlier than you boil or region the water for your filter. This will extend the lifestyles of your filters and could make purifying water that a great deal less difficult.

Boiling the Water

Boiling your water supply is the advocated technique to purify your water. Boiling can kill nearly one hundred% of all microorganisms. We recommend that you boil your water for three-four minutes with the intention to make certain which you completely purify the water. Unfortunately, lighting fixtures a fireplace or the use of a warmth source to simply boil your water is time eating and may drain your gasoline resources.

Chemical Treatment

You should purchase chemical purification pills with the intention to rid water of micro organism, virus, and other problems. These chemical remedy programs are noticeably advise due to their lengthy shelf lifestyles and ease of use. They are also more secure than other techniques we're going to recommend and must be a staple in any preppers deliver kit.

What to Look For In a Filter

Having some transportable filters in your home and in your bug-out-bag is imperative for any prepper. The capacity to clear out water when your water deliver is out can dramatically increase your odds for survival. With that being stated, there are some stuff you must hold in mind while deciding on a filter:

What Is the Filter Made Of?

The filter out medium, or substance that the filter out is comprised of, could have an impact on the overall existence and durability of your clear out. A labyrinth or matrix clear out is a dense filter designed to seize exclusive particles and prevent them from getting into your water. A fiberglass filter out is one of the best filters but has a shorter time frame than different filters. Ceramic filters are frequently the most popular filter out medium. They may be wiped clean multiple times and they seize maximum debris. Unfortunately, they're very delicate and might break effortlessly if you're no longer careful. We suggest which you additionally use a carbon core ceramic clear out as it will capture more particles and better filter out your water.

How Long Will It Last?

Durability is an trouble which you want to be prepared for when selecting a clear out. Some filters will clog or need parts changed earlier than other models. Ceramic filters will commonly closing the longest, however you may lose overall performance after numerous filters. You ought to check the information from the producer as they'll tell you how lengthy a filter have to last. Try to cut this wide variety through 25% or in half of, as it's far better to be secure than sorry. You can constantly amplify the life of your clear out via using a coffee clear out and pre-filtering your water. Sediments and debris will dramatically decrease the shelf lifestyles of your filter out.

How Easy Is It to Clean?

Your filter goes to be grimy and at some point will be clogged. How quickly and without problems the filter out is to easy should be a issue you bear in mind whilst buying the filter out. Once again, ceramic filters are smooth to clean and maintain at some point of their lifespan.

How Much Effort is Required?

Filtering water can require a superb deal of strength, mainly if your clear out has a difficult pump gadget. You can take a look at the manufacturers information which tells you the filter's pump force (i.E., how tough it is to paintings the pump). Other options include gravity filters which rely on gravity to filter the water. These are commonly massive water boxes which you fill and gravity filters. They are in no way portable however they may be a notable addition for your safe house.

UV purifiers

Another alternative that is to be had to you is UV purifiers. These are battery or sun powered purifiers which are simple to apply and very powerful. UV purifiers do not filter out the water, so it is first-rate to have pre-filtered water earlier than the use of your UV cleaner.

Other filters to recollect

Portable aqua

Black Berkeley filter out

Katelyn and Berkeley

Food Storage Tips For Those Who Lack Space

The primary complaint that we listen from new preppers is, "How am I going to save all this meals?" The solution is: with a touch creativity. Many preppers have little to no space available for their food storage supplies so that they motel to finding smart solutions. Before you start to surrender because you don't have any area in your house, take a 2d to get creative. You received't believe how a great deal more space you can find in case you just brainstorm a piece. Keep an open mind and you'll begin to be aware small nooks and crannies as you pass approximately your day-to-day lifestyles in your property. A few cans here, a garage bucket there, this will all upload up and you may speedy locate which you have enough area in your whole meals stockpile.

Remember the Enemies of Food Storage

Just due to the fact you located a small corner or cranny to put a few food in, you need to ensure you it is a safe area for you meals. Small spaces can be exposed to addition warmth, humidity, moisture, and insects. You want to ensure that each location you make a decision to keep your food will prevent infection and is food pleasant for the long haul.

Build a Garage Loft

If you have a excessive ceiling in your storage you should investigate constructing a garage loft. This can be used for storing food, or—even higher—to store objects so that you have more area for your food supply. If you don't have a high ceiling garage, investigate wall shelving. There are numerous corporations focusing on vertical storage garage. Organizing and optimizing your garage will prevent area and allow you to utilize new area for meals storage.

Bathroom Storage

One room that can provide greater storage for exceptional objects is your bathroom. Cabinets, shelving, and small closets can all be used to shop small objects. Try the usage of cabinets to keep the contents below your sink and, alternatively, keep food and water gadgets under your sink.

Empty Suit Cases

Another location that you could shop more meals storage objects is in empty suitcases. Empty suitcases are ideal for food that has been vacuum sealed or saved in Mylar luggage. You can fit quite a bit of emergency food to your suitcases. This also serves as a notable worm-out-bag as you could quickly snatch your suitcase and depart if you are in a hurry. You might be amazed at the quantity of meals and different items you can keep inside the empty suitcases around your own home. We endorse every family member has their own private suitcase that they keep below their mattress. This makes a superb non-public computer virus-out-bag have to you need to evacuate.

Under Or Behind Furniture

You might be surprised at what you may match and save behind or underneath distinctive fixtures gadgets in your property. Many items may be hidden from view so that you received't have numerous ugly buckets or different garage packing containers. But you'll be amazed on the range of vacuum sealed baggage or small packing containers that you can match in random places. Storage here and there can add up quick and you could have quite a large food supply unfold all through your property.

Raising Your Bed

Another place that you may look to save numerous meals and water objects is on top of your refrigerator. Many humans fail to utilize the pinnacle of their refrigerator that can guide a big quantity of food or water. Just recall to put best positive gadgets in your refrigerator until they're one way or the other secured. We endorse maintaining handiest huge items which can be sealed on pinnacle of your refrigerator.

Refrigerator Space

Another region that you could look to keep various meals and water gadgets is on pinnacle of your fridge. Many humans fail to make use of the top in their fridge which could assist a massive amount of food or water. Just don't forget to place only sure gadgets to your fridge unless they're someway secured. We recommend preserving best massive gadgets which are sealed on pinnacle of your fridge.

Canning Introduction

Canning is the best thing ever notion of by mankind. Well, this will be a mild exaggeration, however it is nevertheless quite splendid. It's a first rate way to save your favored ingredients, elements, combos of different recipes, and so much greater, all in sealed jars for maintenance.

What can we suggest via canning? Canning is a manner wherein we seal food or beverages in jars, then warmness them to destroy microorganisms that reason spoilage. It's the same concept that the food enterprise undertakes to position meals, including soups or vegetables, in cans and promote it to the client. With home canning, you're in charge of all of the substances in addition to the flavor and pleasant of your meals.

When we are saying canning we truly imply jarring, but the traditional method of canning receives its name from a meals renovation method brought by way of the French inside the 1800s. We see this carried out these days, all over the world, to canned soups, peaches, beans, and so forth nowadays. The home technique of canning differs in some approaches, however the main principle remains the identical. All canned or jarred foods must be boiled and sealed to some degree to dispose of the unfold of microorganisms.

Home canning is a time examined and powerful technique of meals protection, if you have the right resources. Canned food can be saved for approximately 1 12 months. The blessings to canning are numerous as you could maintain your favourite foods, dispose of waste, and save cash by means of purchasing ingredients in season and keeping them for later.

Canning is a completely precise renovation approach that need to be performed cautiously and with attention to detail as to cast off the risk of any surviving bacteria. However, that doesn't imply that canning is difficult. If you have got the right gear and recipes you can have yourself a canning birthday party in no time. All you need to do is take the proper precautions:

Safety First

Though canning can be a fun and innovative venture, you have to take the proper measures to make sure that the system is performed effectively. Considering the motive of keeping food thru canning is to do away with harmful micro organism, each step must be observed completely to ensure your health and protection. If the jars aren't sterilized or sealed well or boiled at the wrong diploma, you threat contamination. There is no getting it half of right or skipping steps.